Sylvia's

Cakes & Breads

Sylvia's
Cakes & Breads

Famous Recipes
from a Small Maine Kitchen

Sylvia Adams Hocking

Down East Books • Camden / Maine

Down East Books
P.O. Box 679
Camden, ME 04843

This book is dedicated to all my family:

My wonderful parents, Spiro and Jennie Naum Adams, who taught me and my brother, Christy, and sister, Betty, the importance of our Lord in everyday life and the meaning of love, kindness, loyalty, generosity, respect, and integrity. My home teachings have had a very big impact on my life and continue to do so even at the "young" age of 70!

My husband, Arnold True Hocking, who has been part of my lifc for forty-four years.

My son Steven Alan Hocking and his dear wife, Elise, and their four sons (my grandchildren), Christopher, David, Nathan, and Ian.

My son Bryan Timothy Hocking and his dear bride, Janet.

I wish to say thank you to all who made my business, Sylvia's Cakes and Breads, a success and to all my friends who have contributed to my cookbook.

▦ *Contents* ▦

Foreword

I first became acquainted with Sylvia over a cranberry sour cream coffee cake. Some friends of ours sent us this gift at Christmas: a wonderful, gaily decorated cake tin containing the most delicious confection I have ever tasted. My immediate thought was, "My goodness, who made this, and how can I give other people the pleasure that this cake has given me and my family?"

Thus began a long correspondence and friendship, and for ten years or more I have placed orders with Sylvia for Christmas, Valentine's Day, Easter, birthdays, and our own family feasting. I have to confess that though she was not allowed to deliver abroad, I once commissioned a large order from her, and my office sent the cakes to the entire crew of a film I was making in Europe.

Though the cranberry sour cream cake certainly remains a favorite, there are many other wonderful goodies that we have enjoyed: chocolate fudge brownies, applesauce spice cake, pecan pie... anybody who has sampled Sylvia's wares will be devastated to learn that she has retired. Fortunately we have her book and a host of happy memories!

Julie Andrews

Over the years that I was in business, Julie Andrews was my favorite patroness. From the first time she tasted my baked goods, she was a loyal and faithful client, right up to the time of my closing. I thank her for being a big part of Sylvia's Cakes and Breads and bringing great joy to my heart with her artistic and musical abilities. S.A.H.

Some Words from My Friends

When I decided to retire, close the doors of the business, and put together this cook-book of my favorite recipes, I wrote to my many wonderful friends and patrons telling them of my plans. I was so delighted at their response! From all across the country, these faithful customers contacted me with congratulations and offers of help with the book.

I told them that including their memories of Sylvia's Cakes and Breads would be a great addition. Thank you to everyone who took the time to share their thoughts. As you'll see, some of my friends and patrons wrote to me, and others wrote about me. I'm so happy to include all these wonderful memories in my book. S.A.H.

During the last twelve years of Sylvia Adams Hocking's long career, my wife, Judy, and I stayed a bit of each summer and each autumn at our cottage in Rockport, Maine. Every time, we made the pilgrimage to Sylvia's kitchen in South Thomaston to buy fresh berry pies. These visits were always social events, an opportunity to renew our acquaintance with this charming lady and her husband, Arnold. All visits took place in their cozy den, where we would catch up on one another's lives, and where each time we would learn a little more about Sylvia's past growing up on the coast of Maine. Meantime, Arnold would cheerfully contradict her, or agree, or perhaps absent himself to give visiting children a ride on the tractor or a look at the duck pond.

As delightful as these meetings were, what we dreamed about at home in California each winter was summer, marked by a Maine lobster dinner finished with one of Sylvia's fresh two-crust berry pies, preferably blueberry-raspberry. That was our favorite, although we also loved native strawberry and plain wild blueberry. Pecan pie, brownies, coffee cakes—all were wonderful, and all were used for a bit of variety. But for us, nothing in the world could beat Sylvia's berry pies.

Through the years we visited, until Sylvia's retirement, we learned more and more about Sylvia Hocking, but little about how she made her pies, and nothing about how she accomplished her wonderful top crusts. All we were allowed to know had to do with the integrity of her cooking: good ingredients, full measure, and her patient, one-at-a-time technique.

Sylvia is retired now, and I suppose we will never taste her berry pie again. But the chance to try it on our own is at hand, now that she has been persuaded to part with her secrets.

Judy and Steven Levine
Los Angeles, California

Doctors Steven and Judy Levine both have active practices. They have been dear patrons and friends from the very first day they entered my little shop. I always look forward to their visits to Maine.

When we discovered Sylvia and her lemon cake, we solved the hardest problem of all—what to send our good friends for the holidays. We wanted to find something that would make them smile sweetly for several days in a row; something they wouldn't care a hoot if they already had one of; something they would never have to throw away; something that they could with pride share with friends; something they could creep into the kitchen for in the wee hours of the morning; something that was so special that its mysterious pleasure effect couldn't possibly be put into words. That turned out to be—Sylvia's Lemon Cake! Thanks to friends who some time ago sent it to us, we became addicted.

Nan and Dave Grusin
Santa Fe, New Mexico

The Grusins were my patrons for several years, and I have so enjoyed their kind friendship and the many chats on the telephone with Nan. They are both well known in the world of music.

One cold and rainy afternoon in 1989 while location scouting in Maine for a script we were writing, we passed a friendly house with a sign flapping in the wind. It said, "Sylvia's Cakes and Breads." We were chilled to the bone and hungry, so we rang the back door bell. A sweet faced woman welcomed us and we bought two breads: one was prune, the other zucchini. There in the car we devoured them, and then and there we decided that these were to be our Christmas presents to our friends.

We have had Sylvia ship her goods all over the country for the last seven years. Our favorites are her Butter Pound Cake and the Raspberry Buckle. She is the quintessential baker and we are her faithful followers. We wish her continued success in all her endeavors.

Marilyn and Alan Bergman
Beverly Hills, California

The Bergmans have written many of the most memorable and most loved tunes in America today. I'm honored to count them as my special patrons.

xiv

I am at once saddened and yet thrilled with the news of your retirement. In our short relationship you have brought many smiles and happy tummies to my friends. Yours was a labor of love not found on any market shelf.

I trust that you and Mr. Hocking will enjoy retirement together. I look forward to receiving information on your cookbook. The muffin recipe appearing in *Yankee* magazine has been a big hit. The recipe works well with huckleberries, too!

Pete Carroll
Kalispell, Montana

My grandfather, Walter Whitehead, bought Southern Island in Tenants Harbor, Maine, in the early '50s. Each summer, from the time I was born until the island was sold, my family traveled up from Virginia to spend two weeks on Southern Island. My grandfather introduced us to your breads and pies, and it certainly became a tradition to stop at your home and purchase some baked goods. Any trip to Rockland, Thomaston, or Camden would take us by your shop and give us the chance to convince whomever was driving to stop at your home for a purchase.

But, I have other memories of your shop which mean more to me. As a child, I did not know the difference between Southern Island and the state of Maine. I thought Southern Island was Maine, so I would constantly ask, "When are we going to get to Maine?" (even though we had been in Maine for hours). But I knew we were getting close when I saw certain landmarks: a model sailboat in a pond along Route 1 (on the south side of Wiscasset), the two wrecked ships at Wiscasset, and finally your sign, "Sylvia's Cakes and Breads." Then I knew I was real close to Maine.

When I came to Maine as an adult, your sign meant something more; it meant blueberry pie. I tried and tried to convince you to give me your recipe for the crust, but you would always politely decline. I was foolish enough to think my Southern charm would overcome your Yankee stubbornness. My mother purchased one of your blueberry pies and devoured it, by herself, in less than a week. It truly is a Maine tradition.

Now you are writing a cookbook, and I will finally get the recipe. I am sure you are relieved to know that I won't be pestering you anymore. Thanks for the great memories of Maine!

Tom Whitehead
Greensboro, North Carolina

It has truly been a privilege for me to have had the opportunity to meet and know all the Whitehead family; our relationship has gone on for many years. Mr. and Mrs. Whitehead, Tom's grandparents, were regulars in my shop every summer, as were Tom's parents.

We hope it isn't too late for you to use one of these quotes in your cookbook. John and I had some fun last night trying to think of things. This is the one John likes the best: "Sylvia's work is the Currier and Ives of American Bakery."

Here are the others:

"Sylvia's great cakes lift the spirit, like a long-remembered visit to Grandma!"

"Layer by layer, Sylvia's great art really stacks up."

or

"Layer by layer, Sylvia is really stacked!"

We sure are going to miss those cakes. Let us know when the book is ready because I'm really looking forward to the recipes.

Samantha Williams

Los Angeles, California

John and Samantha Williams were a part of the Sylvia's Cakes and Breads mail-order business right from the beginning. For many years, John Williams was the conductor of the Boston Pops, and he has written music scores for many great recent movies. I've been honored to have John and Samantha as my patrons all these many years.

Introduction

I opened the business called Sylvia's Cakes and Breads in 1966 in my home on the St. George Road in South Thomaston, Maine. I started this out of the clear blue sky really for something to do. Our two sons, Steven and Bryan, were ages ten and eleven. My life was partially filled with caring for my family, doing church work, being a member of the Shakespeare Society, taking part in a bridge group, and socializing with our many friends. But somehow I felt a void; I needed to be doing things for many people. I wanted to meet and be with new and varied types of people—to see them smile and be happy because of something I could do.

Food immediately came to mind. My mother always received so much pleasure baking yummy goodies to please all of us and our friends. I remembered my friend, the Right Rev. Ernest Ogden Kenyon of St. Peter's Episcopal Church in Rockland, Maine, my parish priest from the time I was a very young child. He always said bread was the staff of life and that breaking bread together was something we should all do. So one summer afternoon in 1966, I started a batch of bread dough. I made loaves and rolls. I don't remember how many I made, but I know it was more than enough for my family.

I told my two sons to set up a card table on the lawn beside our driveway. I gave them a tablecloth to make it look homey and an "honor jar." I wrapped the cool loaves of bread, and we set them out. The first rolls I made were as hard as a rock. When my husband, Arnold, put them out for the birds, he couldn't wait to tell me, "Even the birds won't eat your rolls."

But that didn't stop me. I made white, oatmeal, wheat, rye, and Nissua breads, plus quick sweet bread and some coffee cakes. It didn't take long for word to get around. The Hart's Neck folks were my best patrons; they told all their friends, and eventually I had to expand my business into my mud room.

One day Maxine Mahoney came in and said to me, "Sylvia, I wish you would make cakes with frosting." So I started doing that, then turning out brownies and many other kinds of squares. Eventually, I was up to around thirty-five or forty different kinds of baked goods. I never had to do any advertising—everything came by word of mouth. All the area's famous artists and their families were my best clients, and many other celebrities were in my shop during the summer months.

Alan and Marilyn Bergman, the writers of many notable musical pieces and movie scores, started me out in my mail-order business. They contacted me (after visiting my shop in the 1980s) to do their Christmas order, and a large one it was. I had no idea how I was going to do this; I didn't have shipping boxes, labels, tins. I didn't have anything! But I did have the ability to get on the phone and find out things in a hurry. That's when I learned how wonderful and helpful people can be. Arnold and I got all the orders out on time. The Bergmans were my patrons for many years, and because of them, many of their friends became my best and most loyal patrons, too.

The mail-order business was very interesting. We started making up brochures, and even though we sent them out only to people who requested one and to people who had already become clients, it was amazing how quickly the word got around. During the holidays, the orders were so great that I had to stop taking more. I was sorry to have to do that, but I could only handle so much work. The last three years of my business, Bryan and his wife, Janet, helped me with all the packing and shipping of the boxes. I'd always done all the baking alone, but the last year, at Christmas time, Bryan helped make brownies. They were the best!

Arnold helped with the shipping and packing at the start of my business, but he eventually lost interest. Besides, I really liked to do everything myself, especially packing some of those gift tins with a special touch for people like Robert Redford and many other well-known figures all over the United States.

My business came to a close on October 31, 1996, because of my arthritis, and perhaps it is for the best. The thirty years of making and selling baked goods were extremely busy ones, but I had no idea how busy until I called it quits. It took me four months to get rested up! I loved every minute of my busy schedule, and to me it never seemed like work. The hundreds of people I have met are the finest in the world. Going into business was the most rewarding experience of a lifetime, and I highly recommend it if you are a people lover with a hidden talent. If I can be of help to anyone starting out, I am more than happy to extend any knowledge gained from my experience. It is very important to me that I and all people be more kind and helpful to one another. Let's all try a little harder and make every day a better one for someone other than ourselves.

I never dreamed my pies or cakes or brownies could reach so many people all over this vast and wonderful country we live in, or that they would make such an impact! Many hours of hard work, mentally and physically, have gone into my thirty-year venture. Caring and giving have been very important to me, and what comes back is so rewarding that all the hard work and many hours seem like happiness to me.

I hope my experience will be an inspiration to some of you. All the letters and telephone calls from so many people everywhere have been a joy to me.

Now my greatest joy is being able to share these great recipes with you, especially all of you who have been enjoying the many baked goods from my Maine kitchen. As Julia Child always says, "*Bon Appétit,*" and as I always say, "Enjoy."

To Preserve a Husband

(contributed by Priscilla Adams-Smith)

"Be careful in your selection; do not choose one too young, and take only such varieties as have been raised in a good moral atmosphere. When once decided upon and selected, let that part remain forever settled and give your entire time and thought to domestic use. Some insist on keeping them in a pickle while others are constantly keeping them in hot water. Even poor varieties may be made sweet, tender and good by garnishing with patience, well sweetened with smiles and flavored with kisses to taste; then wrap them well in a mantle of charity, keep warm with a steady flow of domestic devotion and serve with peaches and cream. When thus prepared they will keep for years."

Mrs. Libby
The Penobscot View Grange Cookbook, circa 1920

A Baker's Dozen of Sylvia's Tips

1. My mother gave me the inspiration to bake. Making a cake, pie, or brownies seemed like such a joyful chore for her that I decided I would like to do baking for pleasure. Her advice to me many, many years ago was to always use the very finest ingredients when cooking and baking—do not substitute. I have always followed that good advice.

2. I am a Grade AA butter user; that came from my mother. There is no substitute when it comes to flavor. The same is true for heavy cream.

3. Pure vanilla flavoring (extract) is a must at all times. Pure flavorings are always best if they are obtainable.

4. My preference in unsweetened cocoa and chocolate baking squares is Hershey's, and I always use REAL chocolate morsels for best flavor.

5. I always buy Gold Medal all-purpose flour for everything except yeast breads, for which I use King Arthur flour.

6. If you don't use cake flour (and I don't), remove one tablespoon of flour from each cupful called for in the recipe.

7. Crisco is my choice for shortening, and I recommend Crisco oil when my recipes call for vegetable oil. I always use Clabber Girl double-acting baking powder. It has never failed me.

8. Top-quality nuts are important to good baking. I ordered mine from Sunnyland Farms in Georgia; they are the very best! (Write to Jane and Harry Willson, Sunnyland Farms, Inc., Albany, GA 31706-8200.)

9. The mixers I use are KitchenAids—both the stand type and a portable model. I also use a Cuisinart for chopping.

10. I prefer stainless-steel loaf pans, cake pans, and cookie sheets. I use solid-bottom tube pans.

11. My favorite cookbook was always *The Betty Crocker Cookbook*, and I also like *Fanny Farmer*, *The Joy of Cooking*, *Better Homes and Gardens*, and Marjorie Standish's two cookbooks, *Cooking Down East* and *Keep Cooking—The Maine Way*. I've also enjoyed the *Southern Living* cookbooks; the Southerners are great cooks. I love Julia Child—her TV shows have been most informative.

12. I think two of the most important steps in baking cakes are thoroughly mixing all the dry ingredients separately and adding them last. In addition, I always test a cake before removing it from the oven, even if the recipe's baking

time has worked fine in the past. I use a metal tester or a toothpick, but either one has to come out absolutely clean before the cake is removed from the oven.

13. This is a tip I think will be helpful to many busy cooks. When you have a baking day and plenty of room in your freezer, make up two or three different flavored pound cakes, using a 10-inch tube pan. Cool the cakes completely, and wrap well before freezing. When you need a cake in a hurry, remove it from the freezer and either cut it in half or into three layers. Make your favorite creamy frosting, and *Voilà!* you have a beautiful layer cake all ready for a birthday or any special occasion. Celebrating is easy when your cake is already baked and ready to be frosted. Pound cakes are not difficult to make and always come out well. The pound cake recipes in this book have never failed me.

▦ Recipes ▦

Cakes

Quick and Easy Chocolate Cake

 This is a very old recipe. Topped with a thick fudge frosting, it was very popular in my shop when I first introduced cakes to my patrons. If you need a yummy dessert in a hurry, this is the one to make. Notice that this recipe doesn't call for any eggs.

In a large bowl, blend well with a mixer at low speed:
   3 cups all-purpose flour
   2 cups sugar
   6 Tbsp. cocoa
   2 tsp. baking soda
   1 tsp. salt

Add:
   $3/4$ cup oil
   2 Tbsp. vinegar
   2 tsp. vanilla

Add last:
   2 cups cold water or coffee

Be sure to grease well the pan or pans you choose. You may also spread waxed paper on the bottom of the pan, then grease the paper before pouring in the thin batter. Bake in a preheated 350° oven for 30 to 40 minutes using either a 13 x 9 x 2-inch pan or two 8 x 8 x 2-inch pans. Test before removing from oven, using a metal cake tester or toothpick. While cake is still warm, spread Sylvia's Chocolate Fudge Frosting (page 9) over the top (or tops).

   This cake is dark and always very moist. It's also delicious served with a generous dollop of whipped cream or ice cream instead of frosting.

Chocolate Cake

Sift together in a large mixing bowl:
    2 cups flour
    2 cups sugar
    3 tsp. baking powder
    1 tsp. salt

Add:
    $^1/_2$ cup soft shortening
    1 $^1/_3$ cups milk

Beat this together on medium speed for two minutes, then add:
    3 eggs
    3 squares unsweetened chocolate, melted
    1 tsp. red food coloring, if desired

Beat for two more minutes, then stir in:
    1 cup chopped nuts.

Pour batter into a well greased 13 x 9 x 2-inch pan, and bake in a pre-heated 350° oven for 40 to 50 minutes.

Devil's Food Cake

 This recipe was given to me by my mother, Jennie Adams, many years ago. It's a little bit more complicated than the average chocolate cake, but it is well worth the effort if you have the time.

Cream together well:
    1 stick butter ($^1/_2$ cup)
    1 cup sugar
    1 cup firmly packed light brown sugar
Add:
    3 squares unsweetened chocolate, melted and slightly cooled
Add:
    6 large egg yolks
Beat well with:
    3 Tbsp. cold water using a wire whisk or fork

Sift together and add:
    2 cups cake flour
    1 tsp. baking soda
    $^{1}/_{2}$ tsp. salt
Alternately with:
    1 cup buttermilk
    1 tsp. vanilla

Beat together until well blended. Pour into two greased 9-inch layer pans, and bake in a preheated 350° oven for 30 to 35 minutes or until done.

Leave cakes in pans for about 10 minutes before turning out onto cake rack. Do not frost until cakes are cold. My mother used boiled frosting; I prefer my Fluffy Butter Cream Frosting (page 8) and like to put chocolate sprills over the top.

Note: If you don't use cake flour (and I don't), remove 1 Tbsp. of flour from each cupful called for in the recipe.

Easy Devil's Food Cake

 Here's an easy chocolate cake. It's a nice one to serve at home or to take as a treat to someone's house.

Cream together well:
    $^{1}/_{2}$ cup butter or margarine
    1 $^{1}/_{2}$ cups sugar
Add, one at a time:
    2 large eggs
    1 tsp. vanilla
    $^{1}/_{4}$ tsp. salt
Sift together and add:
    2 $^{1}/_{4}$ cups all-purpose flour
    1 $^{1}/_{4}$ tsp. baking soda
    $^{1}/_{2}$ cup cocoa
Alternately with:
    1 $^{1}/_{2}$ cups buttermilk
Beat in until well mixed.

Using a 350° preheated oven, bake in a well buttered 13 x 9 x 2-inch pan for 40 minutes; a well buttered 10-inch tube or bundt pan for 40 to 50 minutes; or two well buttered 8-inch layer pans for 25 to 35 minutes.

Nana's Chocolate Cake

 This is another chocolate cake recipe from my mother. By now, you have probably realized that the Adams family loved chocolate cakes and enjoyed making many different recipes.

In a large bowl, mix:
    2^1/$_2$ cups all-purpose flour
    ^{3}/$_4$ tsp. salt
    4 tsp. baking soda
    ^{2}/$_3$ cup cocoa
    2 cups sugar
Add:
    3 eggs
    ^{3}/$_4$ cup oil
    2 cups buttermilk
    1^1/$_2$ tsp. vanilla
Beat on high speed for two minutes.

Pour into a greased and floured tube or bundt pan. Bake in a preheated 350° oven for 40 to 50 minutes. Cake may also be baked in a buttered, floured 13 x 9 x 2-inch pan for 40 to 50 minutes.

Nana's Fudge Cake

 I found this recipe in one of my mother's oldest cookbooks. As my sons can attest, she made yummy cakes.

    2 squares unsweetened baking chocolate
    ^{1}/$_2$ cup hot water
    1^1/$_2$ cups firmly packed light brown sugar
    ^{1}/$_2$ cup butter
    4 large eggs
    ^{1}/$_2$ cup sour milk (or buttermilk)
    1 tsp. vanilla
    1^3/$_4$ cups all-purpose flour
    ^{1}/$_2$ tsp. baking soda
    1 tsp. salt

Cut chocolate into small pieces and add the hot water. Allow to melt. Cream sugar, butter, and eggs together until fluffy. Add the sour milk and vanilla. Sift flour, baking soda, and salt together, and blend into the creamed mixture. Add the melted chocolate, and mix thoroughly. Pour into a well buttered 13 x 9 x 2-inch pan, and bake in a preheated 325° oven for 45 minutes or until done. (You can also bake this cake in a 9-inch tube pan.) Frost with Sylvia's Chocolate Fudge Frosting (page 9).

Frosted Chocolate Sheet Cake

Put in saucepan and bring to a boil:
- 1 stick margarine or butter
- $1/2$ cup oil
- 4 Tbsp. unsweetened cocoa
- 1 cup water

In large bowl, place:
- 2 cups all-purpose flour
- 2 cups sugar

Mix on low until blended. Pour cocoa mixture over dry ingredients, and blend well.

Add:
- $1/2$ cup buttermilk
- 2 eggs
- 1 tsp. baking soda
- 1 tsp. vanilla

Pour into large, greased jelly-roll pan. Bake 20 minutes in preheated 400° oven. While cake is baking, prepare frosting:

Frosting

- 1 stick butter or margarine
- 4 Tbsp. cocoa
- $1/3$ cup buttermilk
- 1 pound confectioners' sugar
- $1/2$ tsp. salt
- 1 tsp. vanilla
- 1 cup chopped nuts

Bring butter, cocoa, and buttermilk just to a boil. Remove from heat. Add remaining ingredients and blend. Apply frosting while cake is hot. When cool, cut into 30 large squares.

Chocolate Layer Cake

 This was a favorite of my three "boys": my husband, Arnold, and my sons, Steven and Bryan. I used to make it all the time during the 1960s, with the frosting that follows the cake recipe.

$^1/_2$ cup shortening
1 $^1/_2$ cups sugar
2 extra-large eggs
$^1/_4$ cup water
3 Tbsp. cocoa
1 tsp. salt (scant)

2 $^1/_2$ cups all-purpose flour
1 cup buttermilk
1 tsp. vanilla
1 tsp. vinegar
1 tsp. baking soda

In a large bowl, cream shortening, sugar, and eggs. Make a paste of water and cocoa. Add to the creamed mixture. With mixer, add salt, flour, buttermilk, and vanilla. Stir in (don't beat) vinegar and baking soda. Bake in two greased 9-inch layer pans in a preheated 350° oven for 30 to 35 minutes.

Butter Frosting:

Heat in a saucepan, stirring constantly until thickened:

    3 Tbsp. flour
    1 cup water

Allow to cool, then cream together:

    1 cup confectioners' sugar
    1 cup (2 sticks) butter or margarine
    1 tsp. vanilla

Blend until sugar is dissolved, then add the cooled, cooked mixture and mix well; beat in a mixer or with an electric beater until thick, about 10 minutes.

Rich and Delicious Fudge Cake

In large bowl, cream together:
   $2/3$ cup butter
   $1^3/4$ cups sugar
   2 eggs
   1 tsp. vanilla
Beat with mixer for 5 minutes at high speed, then melt:
   $2^1/2$ squares unsweetened chocolate.
Add to creamed mixture and beat well.

Sift together:
   $2^1/2$ cups cake flour
   $1^1/4$ tsp. baking soda
   $1/2$ tsp. salt
Add to creamed mixture alternately with:
   $1^1/4$ cups ice water

Thoroughly grease two 9-inch layer pans, pour in batter, and bake in a preheated 350° oven for 30 to 35 minutes. Frost and fill with Sylvia's Creamy Mocha Frosting (page 51) or whipped cream.

Note: If you don't use cake flour, leave out 3 Tbsp. of all-purpose flour from the total; it works very well.

Quick and Easy Cocoa Cake

$2^1/2$ cups flour   1 cup milk
$1^3/4$ cups sugar $2/3$ cup butter or margarine
$1/2$ cup unsweetened cocoa   2 tsp. vanilla
2 tsp. baking soda   3 eggs
$1/2$ tsp. salt

Heat oven to 350°. Grease well and flour a 13 x 9 x 2-inch pan. In large mixing bowl, combine all ingredients. Beat 1 minute at low speed to combine ingredients, then beat for 3 minutes at highest speed. Pour batter into prepared pan. Bake for 35 to 45 minutes or until done. This cake is good with Sylvia's Chocolate Fudge Frosting (page 9).

Cocoa Party Cake

 This makes a nice layer cake, especially when covered with my Fluffy Butter Cream Frosting below.

1 cup butter	2^3/4 cups cake flour
2^3/4 cups sugar	^{1}/2 cup cocoa
2 tsp. vanilla	2 tsp. baking soda
1 tsp. salt	2 cups buttermilk
2 eggs	

Combine butter and sugar, adding vanilla and salt. Beat until creamy. Add the eggs, one at a time. Sift together flour, cocoa, and baking soda, then add these to the creamed mixture alternately with the buttermilk. Grease and flour two 9-inch square pans. Pour batter into pans and bake in a pre-heated 350° oven for 30 to 35 minutes or until done.

Sylvia's Fluffy Butter Cream Frosting:

1 egg
1 stick butter
1 heaping cup white Crisco (no substitute)
^{1}/4 tsp. salt
2 lb. confectioners' sugar
2 tsp. vanilla
^{1}/2 tsp. almond extract
^{1}/4 cup heavy cream or milk (use more or less, as needed)

Cream together the egg, butter, Crisco, and salt until you've got a mayonnaise-like consistency. Add the confectioners' sugar, extracts, and milk or cream, and beat on low speed until completely blended. Beat on medium for 10 minutes. Keep checking to see if the frosting needs more cream or more sugar. It should be fluffy—like whipped cream—and just right for spreading. This will frost one large layer cake or the tops of two tube cakes.

For mocha frosting:

Add 4 squares melted unsweetened baking chocolate, and substitute hot coffee for the cream.

For maple pecan frosting:

Add 2 Tbsp. maple extract (instead of almond) 1 tsp. vanilla, and—at the end—1^1/2 cups toasted pecans.

Chocolate Fudge Cake

 This cake was very popular with my customers. I covered it with thick, Sylvia's Creamy Mocha Frosting (page 51), with Sylvia's Chocolate Fudge Frosting, below, or with Sylvia's Fluffy Butter Cream Frosting (page 8). I usually topped it off with chocolate sprills. The tube cakes may be cut through the middle, then filled and frosted as you would a layer cake. Yummy!

3$^1/_2$ cups flour	2 cups buttermilk or sour milk
3 cups sugar	I cup shortening
$^2/_3$ cup cocoa	3 tsp. vanilla
2$^1/_2$ tsp. baking soda	4 extra-large eggs
2 tsp. salt	

In a large bowl, place the flour, sugar, cocoa, baking soda, and salt. Beat with a mixer on the lowest speed until completely blended. Add the buttermilk, shortening, and vanilla; beat on medium speed for 2 minutes. Add the 4 eggs all at once, and blend in for about 30 seconds on low speed; then beat on medium speed for 2 minutes. Divide this batter between two buttered tube pans, and bake in a preheated 350° oven for 45 to 50 minutes or until done. Do not overbake.

Sylvia's Chocolate Fudge Frosting:

Note: This will frost the tops of two large cakes. If you're going to cut the cakes into layers and want to frost the sides and middles, as well, Creamy Mocha Frosting or Sylvia's Fluffy Butter Cream Frosting are better choices.

Melt together in large saucepan:
  3 squares unsweetened chocolate
  4 Tbsp. butter
  2 Tbsp. corn syrup (light or dark)
  $^1/_8$ tsp. salt

Stir constantly to keep mixture from sticking to bottom of pan. Remove from burner when all is melted, then add:
  2 cups (or more) confectioners' sugar or a 1-lb. box
  2 tsp. vanilla
  2 to 4 Tbsp. (or more) very hot coffee or water

Mix until very smooth and thick enough to spread over tops of cakes (work quickly). If frosting seems too thick, just add more liquid, and if it seems too thin, just add more confectioners' sugar. You can't spoil this! It's just a great, easy-to-make frosting.

Chocolate Swirl Cake

In large mixing bowl, beat together on medium speed:
   2 sticks butter or margarine, softened
   2 cups sugar
   2 tsp. vanilla
   $^1/_2$ tsp. salt
Add one at a time, blending well:
   3 eggs
Mix together:
   $2^3/_4$ cups flour
   1 tsp. baking soda
Add this alternately to creamed mixture with:
   1 cup buttermilk or sour milk

Remove 2 cups vanilla batter to a medium sized bowl. In a separate, smaller bowl, combine 1 cup chocolate syrup and $^1/_4$ tsp. baking soda; blend into the 2 cups batter. Add optional 1 cup coconut to remaining vanilla batter in original large mixing bowl. Pour into well greased 10-inch tube pan. Pour chocolate batter over vanilla batter. Do not stir—it will swirl while baking. Bake in a preheated 350° oven for about 70 minutes. Cool in pan for 15 minutes. Turn out of pan and cool completely. Spoon or pour chocolate frosting over cake.

Note: If you don't have buttermilk or sour milk for the cake, add 2 tsp. vinegar to 1 cup plain milk, stir, and let it set for about 5 to 10 minutes until slightly thickened.

Chocolate Frosting:

In a saucepan, combine:
   2 Tbsp. water
   2 tsp. light corn syrup
   2 squares unsweetened chocolate
Heat chocolate until melted. Remove from burner.

Add:
   $1^1/_2$ cups confectioners' sugar, stirring for about 1 minute.

Stir in:
   $^1/_4$ tsp. vanilla

If frosting becomes too thick, add hot water.

Chocolate-Vanilla Swirl Cake

2 cups chocolate bits
1 cup butter, softened
1 $^1/_2$ cups sugar
1 Tbsp. vanilla
4 eggs

2 $^1/_2$ cups flour
2 tsp. baking powder
$^1/_2$ tsp. salt
1 cup milk
1 cup chopped pecans

Melt chocolate bits over hot (not boiling) water; remove from heat and cool. In a large bowl, cream the butter and sugar well; add vanilla and eggs, one at a time. Mix together the flour, baking powder, and salt; add to the creamed mixture alternately with the milk. Mix until all is well combined.

Divide batter in half. Stir melted chocolate into one half of the batter, and blend the chopped pecans into the other. Alternately layer batters into a greased 10-inch fluted or plain tube pan.

Bake in a preheated 375° oven for 60 to 70 minutes. Cool for 10 minutes, and remove from pan. Dust top with confectioners' sugar.

Cocoa Fudge Cake

 This is a recipe I've had for many years. It's a nice cake, and it will serve sixteen people, so it's a good one to take to a picnic or a party.

$^3/_4$ cup unsweetened cocoa
$^3/_4$ cup boiling water or coffee
$^1/_4$ cup butter
$^1/_4$ cup shortening
2 cups sugar
$^1/_8$ tsp. salt

2 eggs
1 tsp. vanilla
1 $^1/_2$ tsp. baking soda
1 cup buttermilk
1 $^3/_4$ cups all-purpose unsifted
   flour

Make a smooth paste of the cocoa and water or coffee. Cool slightly. Cream butter, shortening, sugar, and salt until fluffy. Beat in eggs one at a time, beating well. Add vanilla. Stir baking soda into buttermilk. Add alternately to creamed mixture with flour. Add cocoa/water mixture, and blend thoroughly.

Pour into a greased 13 x 9 x 2-inch pan and bake for 40 to 45 minutes in a preheated 350° oven.

Chocolate Cake with Fudge Frosting

Melt together:
   1/2 cup butter
   6 Tbsp. cocoa
Pour into large mixing bowl and add:
   2 cups sugar
   2 large eggs
   2 tsp. baking soda
   1/2 tsp. salt
   2 tsp. vanilla
   3 cups all-purpose flour
   2 cups buttermilk

Beat with mixer until all ingredients are thoroughly combined.

   Grease well two 8 x 8 x 2-inch square pans or two 9 x 9 x 2-inch square pans for a layer cake, or two 9 x 5 x 3-inch pans for loaf cakes. Pour in batter, and bake in a preheated 350° oven for 35 to 45 minutes.

Fudge Frosting:

Melt in medium size saucepan:
   3 squares unsweetened chocolate
   1/2 stick butter (1/4 cup)
   1/8 tsp. salt
   1 Tbsp. corn syrup
Add:
   1/2 cup sugar
   1/3 cup milk
Boil for 2 to 3 minutes. Cool slightly, then add:
   2 generous cups confectioners' sugar
   2 tsp. vanilla

Stir well until thick enough to spread. Add more confectioners' sugar if too thin or more milk (heated) if too thick.

Chocolate Chiffon Cake

 My dear daughter-in-law Elise Hocking, Steve's wife, sent this from Beavercreek, Ohio.

¹/₂ cup cocoa	1 tsp. salt
³/₄ cup boiling water	¹/₂ cup oil
1³/₄ cups cake flour	7 eggs, separated
1³/₄ cups sugar	2 tsp. vanilla
1¹/₂ tsp. baking soda	¹/₄ tsp. cream of tartar

In a small bowl, mix cocoa and water until smooth; cool for 20 minutes. In a mixing bowl, combine flour, sugar, baking soda, and salt. Add oil, egg yolks, vanilla, and cocoa mixture; beat until smooth. In another mixing bowl, beat egg whites and cream of tartar until stiff peaks form. Gradually fold in egg yolk mixture. Pour into an ungreased 10-inch tube pan. Bake on lowest rack in a preheated 325° oven for 60 to 65 minutes or until cake springs back when touched. Invert pan to cool; remove cake from pan.

Note from Elise: "I do not use cake flour. . . . I use unbleached flour. I converted the measurements by subtracting 3¹/₂ Tbsp. of the flour out of the 1³/₄ cups total."

Frosting:

¹/₃ cup butter or margarine	1¹/₂ tsp. vanilla
2 squares unsweetened chocolate	3 to 4 Tbsp. hot water
2 cups confectioners' sugar	chopped nuts, optional

Melt butter and chocolate together in medium saucepan. Remove from heat; stir in sugar and vanilla. Add water until frosting is of desired consistency; drizzle over cake. Sprinkle with nuts. Yield: 16 to 20 servings.

Krista's Chocolate Cheese Delight

Cake:

Mix together in a large bowl:

    1 $\frac{1}{2}$ cups flour

    1 cup sugar

    $\frac{1}{4}$ cup unsweetened cocoa

    1 tsp. baking soda

Add and mix together:

    1 cup water

    $\frac{1}{3}$ cup oil

    1 Tbsp. vinegar

    1 tsp. vanilla

Pour batter into a greased 9 x 9 x 2-inch pan.

Topping:

Mix together:

    1 (8 oz.) pkg. cream cheese, softened

    1 egg

    $\frac{1}{8}$ tsp. salt

    $\frac{1}{4}$ cup sugar

    1 cup chocolate bits

    1 tsp. vanilla

Drop by teaspoonfuls over cake batter.

Sprinkle sugar and chopped nuts on top before baking. Place pan in a preheated 350° oven for 35 minutes or until done.

Silver White Cake

2 $\frac{1}{4}$ cups sifted cake flour	$\frac{1}{2}$ cup shortening
1 $\frac{1}{2}$ cups sugar	1 cup milk
3 $\frac{1}{2}$ tsp. baking powder	1 $\frac{1}{2}$ tsp. vanilla or part almond extract
1 tsp. salt	4 egg whites

Into large bowl, sift flour with sugar, baking powder, and salt. Add shortening, milk, and vanilla. Mix ingredients on low speed until completely combined. On medium speed, beat for 2 minutes. Add unbeaten egg whites; beat 2 minutes longer.

Pans should be well greased and floured. Pour into either two 8-inch cake pans, a 13 x 9 x 2-inch oblong pan, or a 9-inch tube pan. In preheated 350° oven, bake layers 30 to 35 minutes, oblong loaf 35 to 40 minutes, or tube cake 50 minutes.

White Layer Cake with Lemon Filling

2^1/4 cups flour
1^2/3 cups sugar
3^1/2 tsp. baking powder
1 tsp. salt
^{2}/3 cup shortening

1^1/4 cups milk
1^1/2 tsp. vanilla
^{1}/2 tsp. almond extract (optional)
5 egg whites

Grease and flour two 9 x 9 x 2-inch square pans. In a large bowl, combine flour, sugar, baking powder, salt, shortening, milk, and flavoring; beat for 30 seconds with mixer on low speed, scraping bowl constantly. Beat 2 minutes on high speed, scraping bowl occasionally. Add egg whites, and beat on high speed for 2 more minutes. Pour into pans. Bake in a preheated 350° oven 30 to 35 minutes.

Lemon Filling:

^{3}/4 cup sugar
3 Tbsp. cornstarch
^{1}/4 tsp. salt
^{3}/4 cup water

1 tsp. grated lemon peel
1 Tbsp. butter or margarine
^{1}/3 cup lemon juice
4 drops yellow food coloring, if desired

Mix sugar, cornstarch, and salt in saucepan. Stir in water gradually. Cook, stirring constantly, until mixture thickens and boils. Boil and stir 5 minutes. Remove from heat; add lemon peel and butter. Stir in lemon juice and food coloring, if desired; cool. If filling is too soft, refrigerate until set. Spread evenly over bottom layer of cake, and top with second layer.

Whip about 1 pint heavy cream with a couple of tablespoons confectioners' sugar and 1 tsp. vanilla. Frost the top and sides of the cake. This is a delicious cake, and it's especially nice for parties.

Vanilla Cake

 This makes a nice birthday cake done either in layers or as a 10-inch tube cake. finish it off with Sylvia's Fluffy Butter Cream Frosting (page 8).

2 cups plus 2 Tbsp. flour
1 1/2 cups sugar
2 extra-large eggs
3 tsp. baking powder
1 tsp. salt

1/2 cup shortening
1 cup milk
1 1/2 tsp. vanilla
1/4 tsp. (or more) almond extract

Combine all ingredients except eggs in large mixing bowl; beat for 2 minutes. Add eggs, and beat for 2 more minutes.

Preheat oven to 350°. Grease and flour one 10-inch tube pan (bake 40 to 50 minutes) or two 8-inch layer pans (bake 30 to 35 minutes) or one 13 x 9 x 2-inch pan (bake 35 to 40 minutes). Pour batter into pan or pans, and bake accordingly.

Note: For lemon cake, use 1 1/2 tsp. lemon flavoring instead of vanilla, and add grated rind. Frost with Sylvia's Fluffy Butter Cream Frosting (page 8) substituting lemon extract for the vanilla and almond extracts.

Cream Cake with Spanish Sauce

Cream Cake:

2 eggs
1 cup sugar
1 cup cream

2 cups flour
1 tsp. baking soda
1 tsp. cream of tartar

Mix all together, place in a 9 x 9 x 2-inch greased baking pan, and bake in a preheated 350° oven for 30 minutes. Serve with

Spanish Sauce:

1/2 cup water
1 Tbsp. cornstarch
1 tsp. vinegar
3 Tbsp. butter

1 cup sugar (or less)
1/4 tsp. nutmeg
1 tsp. lemon extract

Mix all ingredients, and cook over low heat until thickened.

Sponge Cake

9 eggs
2 cups sugar
2 cups flour

3 tsp. baking powder
$1/4$ tsp. baking soda

Beat eggs for 2 minutes; add sugar to mixture, and beat for 4 minutes. Add remaining ingredients, and beat for 5 minutes on medium speed. Pour batter into an ungreased 13 x 9 x 2-inch pan and bake in a pre-heated 350° oven for 45 minutes or until light brown. When cake is cool, cut into diamond shapes, and pour warm syrup over it.

Syrup:

$2^1/2$ cups sugar
3 cups water

$1/8$ tsp. nutmeg
juice of one lemon

Simmer together for 10 minutes (sugar should melt). Add the lemon juice, and cool slightly before pouring over cake.

Granny's Sponge Cakes

 This recipe was a childhood favorite of my friend Martha Lord. She always looked forward to receiving a "care package" of these cakes when she was away at school. Martha says her aunt's cook could make them so they almost floated. This is a very old recipe, originating at least 85 years ago.

5 eggs, separated and at room temperature
1 cup sifted confectioners' sugar
rind and juice of $1/2$ lemon
2 Tbsp. cold water
$3/4$ cup sifted cake flour
1 tsp. double acting baking powder

Beat egg yolks very hard; combine sugar with lemon rind, and add to eggs. Beat again. Beat in lemon juice and cold water. Sift flour with baking powder and fold in. Fold in beaten egg whites.

Preheat oven to 325°. Pour batter into greased or lined muffin tins, sprinkle with sugar, and place in oven. Immediately turn up temperature to 350°. Bake for about 25 to 35 minutes. Be sure to check for doneness with metal cake tester or toothpick. Makes 12 cakes.

Lemon Glaze Cake

 This was always a favorite cake at my bakery shop. Sometimes, instead of using the soaked-in glaze, I would put a thick, creamy lemon frosting on top.

In large mixing bowl, beat for two minutes:
  $4^1/_4$ cups all-purpose flour
  3 cups sugar
  2 Tbsp. baking powder (6 tsp.)
  2 tsp. salt
  1 cup shortening
  2 cups milk
  1 Tbsp. lemon extract (3 tsp.)
Add:
  4 extra-large eggs
Beat for two more minutes.

Pour into two greased 10-inch tube pans and bake in a preheated 350° oven for 40 to 50 minutes. This recipe will also fill four 8-inch layer pans (bake for 25 to 35 minutes) or three loaf pans (bake for 35 to 45 minutes). Use these sizes to plan amount of frosting.

Lemon Glaze
(enough for two large tube cakes):
Mix:
  2 (8 oz.) containers or 1 (16 oz.) container frozen lemonade
    concentrate, thawed
  2 to 3 cups sugar

Blend thoroughly, and stir together occasionally while cakes are baking.
  As soon as cakes are removed from oven, prick all over with a large meat fork and loosen cakes around sides and center tube. With a long-handled ladle, spoon glaze over the two cakes, which will soak up the liquid. As soon as all the glaze has soaked in (about 10 minutes), sprinkle lightly with sugar, turn out of the pan onto a cake rack, then turn right-side up. Sprinkle all over again with sugar—a little heavier this time—to make a crunchy top.

Glazed Orange Loaf Cake

 This is a delicious cake—quick and easy to prepare. My mother used to make this and I loved it! It's a very nice "tea party" cake.

2 cups cake flour	$^{1}/_{2}$ cup orange juice (fresh)
1 cup sugar	$^{1}/_{2}$ cup shortening
1 $^{1}/_{2}$ tsp. baking powder	2 eggs
$^{1}/_{2}$ tsp. salt	2 Tbsp. grated orange peel (optional)

Sift all dry ingredients into mixing bowl, and add remaining ingredients except for the eggs and optional grated orange peel. Beat with mixer for 2 minutes on medium speed. Add the unbeaten eggs and orange peel (if desired), and beat for 2 more minutes. Pour batter into a greased 8 x 4 x 3-inch loaf pan, and bake for 45 to 55 minutes in a preheated 350° oven.

Glaze:

$^{1}/_{4}$ cup orange juice (fresh)
$^{1}/_{2}$ cup confectioners' sugar (or more)

Mix together to glaze consistency and drizzle over cake.

One Egg Cake

1 cup sugar	2 tsp. baking powder
$^{1}/_{2}$ cup shortening	$^{1}/_{4}$ tsp. baking soda
1 egg	$^{1}/_{2}$ tsp. salt
$^{1}/_{2}$ tsp. lemon flavoring	1 cup buttermilk or sour milk
$^{1}/_{2}$ tsp. vanilla	$^{1}/_{2}$ cup chocolate bits
2 cups flour	$^{1}/_{2}$ cup shredded coconut or chopped walnuts

Cream together sugar, shortening, egg, and flavorings. Sift flour, baking powder, baking soda, and salt; add alternately to creamed mixture with sour milk. Mix until well blended.

Sprinkle top of cake with the chocolate bits and/or coconut or walnuts. Bake in a greased 9 x 9 x2-inch pan in a preheated 350° oven for 40 minutes.

Lizzie's Applesauce Cake

 This recipe was given to me by my mother-in-law, Gladys Hocking, when Arnold and I first got married. Many years ago, I made this cake in a 9-inch-square pan, covered it with butter frosting, sprinkled chopped walnuts on top, and gave it to my brother, Judge Christy C. Adams. It became his favorite cake because of its delicious flavor. I usually doubled the recipe so we would have an extra one to share.

Blend together in a large mixing bowl:
   1 cup shortening
   1 tsp. salt
   1 tsp. cinnamon
   1 tsp. nutmeg
   $^1/_2$ tsp. cloves
   1 tsp. allspice
   4 Tbsp. cocoa

Add:
   3 cups sugar, creaming well
   4 eggs, unbeaten, one at a time
   3 tsp. soda
   4 cups all-purpose flour
   3 cups unsweetened applesauce

Beat together on low until well blended, then beat on medium speed for about two minutes.

Stir in:
   2 to 3 cups raisins (during the holidays, I like to substitute whole red
      cherries)

Pour into two bundt pans, or two 10-inch tube pans, or two 9 x 9 x 2-inch pans, or three 9 x 5 x 3-inch loaf pans—each well greased and floured on the bottom. Bake in a preheated 350° oven for 40 to 55 minutes or until done. Be sure to test.

Applesauce Spice Cake

 This was a big favorite both in my shop and among my mail-order customers.

Blend on low speed in a large mixing bowl:
   2 1/2 cups flour
   2 cups sugar
   1 1/2 tsp. salt
   1 1/2 tsp. baking soda
   1/4 tsp. baking powder
   1 tsp. cinnamon
   1/2 tsp. cloves
   1/2 tsp. nutmeg
   1/2 tsp. allspice

Add to this:
   1 1/2 cups applesauce
   1/2 cup Crisco
   1/2 cup water
Mix on low, then beat on medium speed for 2 minutes.

Add:
   2 extra-large eggs
Beat for 2 more minutes.

Fold in last:
   1 cup raisins
   1/2 cup chopped walnuts

Grease and flour a 10-inch tube pan or two 9 x 5 x 3-inch loaf pans. Pour in batter, and bake in a preheated 350° oven for 55 to 60 minutes.

Nana's Applesauce Cake

 This is another recipe I found on a card tucked into my mother's oldest cookbook. When I tried it, we all thought it was quite delicious.

In large bowl, cream together until fluffy:

   $^1/_2$ cup (1 stick) butter, softened

   1 $^1/_2$ cups sugar

Add:

   3 large eggs, one at a time

Sift dry ingredients:

   2 cups all-purpose flour

   2 tsp. baking soda

   1 tsp. cinnamon

   $^1/_2$ tsp. cloves

   $^1/_2$ tsp. nutmeg

   $^1/_2$ tsp. salt

Add:

   1 cup chopped dates

   $^1/_2$ cup chopped nuts

Alternately add the dry ingredients to the creamed mixture with:

   1 $^1/_2$ cups applesauce

Mix thoroughly, then turn into a well buttered tube or bundt pan, and bake in preheated 325° oven for about 1 hour or until done.

Note: This cake may be served as is or with Butter Frosting or Caramel Frosting.

Mrs. Withington's Applesauce Cake

$^1/_2$ cup shortening

2 cups sugar

1 large egg

1 $^1/_2$ cups unsweetened applesauce

2 tsp. baking soda

$^1/_2$ cup boiling water

2 $^1/_2$ cups flour

$^1/_2$ tsp. salt

$^1/_2$ tsp. cinnamon

$^1/_2$ tsp. cloves

$^1/_2$ tsp. allspice

1 cup seeded raisins

1 cup dates, cut in half

Cream shortening and add sugar gradually. Add egg and applesauce. Put baking soda in boiling water, and add to creamed mixture. Sift together flour, salt, and spices and add to mixture. Flour the raisins and dates thoroughly with an extra 2 Tbsp. flour, and add to the cake batter. Cut-up candied cherries and nuts can be added if desired.

Bake in two well greased $8^1/_2$ x 4 x 3-inch loaf pans. Bake in a preheated 350° oven for about 1 hour.

My Mother's Spice Cake

$^1/_2$ cup shortening
$1^1/_2$ cups firmly packed brown sugar
2 eggs, well beaten
$2^3/_4$ cups flour
1 tsp. cinnamon
1 tsp. nutmeg
$^1/_2$ tsp. cloves
$^1/_2$ tsp. salt
2 tsp. baking powder
$^1/_2$ tsp. baking soda
1 cup sour milk
1 cup raisins, chopped (optional)

Cream shortening and sugar. Add eggs. Beat thoroughly. Sift flour, measure it, and sift together with spices, salt, baking powder, and baking soda. Add dry ingredients to creamed mixture alternately with milk. Beat thoroughly. If desired, add raisins, dredging first in 2 Tbsp. flour. Pour into greased layer-cake pans. Bake in a preheated 350° oven for 30 to 40 minutes. (This cake can also be baked in a 13 x 9 x 2-inch greased pan for 40 to 50 minutes.) Cover with either White Mountain Frosting (page 55) or Satiny Beige Frosting (page 55), and sprinkle with crushed walnuts.

Buttermilk Spice Cake

2 cups sifted cake flour
1 cup sugar
$^3/_4$ cup firmly packed brown sugar
1 tsp. baking powder
$^3/_4$ tsp. baking soda
1 tsp. salt
1 tsp. cinnamon
$^1/_4$ tsp. cloves
$^1/_2$ cup shortening
1 cup buttermilk
3 eggs

In large bowl, place flour, sugars, baking powder, baking soda, salt, and spices. Mix together well. Add shortening and buttermilk, and beat with mixer for 2 minutes on medium speed. Add the 3 eggs, and beat for 2 more minutes.

Pour into a greased 9- or 10-inch tube pan, or, if you want to make a layer cake, into two greased 9 x 9 x 2-inch square pans. Bake in a pre-heated 350° oven for 40 to 50 minutes. This is good with Easy Penuche Frosting, below, or Satiny Beige Frosting (page 55).

Easy Penuche Frosting:

$^1/_2$ cup butter
1 cup brown sugar
$^1/_4$ cup milk
$2^1/_2$ cups confectioners' sugar

Melt butter in saucepan. Stir in brown sugar. Bring to a boil; cook and stir over low heat for 2 minutes. Stir in milk. Return to a boil, stirring constantly. Remove from heat and cool to lukewarm (120°). Gradually beat in confectioners' sugar.

Mrs. Ramsdell's Blueberry Cake

 Mrs. Rena Ramsdell gave me this recipe way back in the 1950s. I first made this cake at the summer cottage of my husband's family. It was fun to bake there—the kitchen was huge! The recipe was always a big hit with Arnold's family. I later made this cake as a blueberry butter buckle when I opened my shop. It was very popular with my customers.

In large mixing bowl, cream together well:

$^1/_2$ cup shortening

1 $^1/_2$ cups sugar

2 extra-large eggs

1 tsp. salt

1 $^1/_2$ tsp. vanilla

Add:

3 cups all-purpose flour

3 tsp. (mounded) baking powder

Alternately with:

1 cup milk

Beat until all is well blended. Put a handful of flour onto a plate, and dredge 3 cups of blueberries in it. Fold the berries into the cake batter. Pour into well buttered 13 x 9 x 2-inch pan. Before baking, sprinkle the top with sugar or the following.

Topping:

Mix with a fork until crumbly:

$^1/_2$ cup brown sugar

$^1/_2$ cup flour

$^1/_4$ cup soft butter

$^1/_2$ tsp. cinnamon

Bake in a preheated 350° oven for 45 minutes or until baked; use a cake tester or toothpick to make sure.

Note: This cake is also delicious when baked in a 10-inch tube pan. To decorate, cover with cream-cheese frosting and sprinkle with toasted pecans. I even made it this way for a few weddings.

Buttermilk Blueberry Cake

Cream together well:
   2 cups sugar
   1 cup shortening
   2 extra-large eggs
   1 tsp. salt
   2 tsp. vanilla
Mix together or sift:
   4 cups all-purpose flour
   1 tsp. baking soda
Add alternately to creamed mixture with:
   1 ^{1}/$_3$ cups buttermilk
Beat together until well blended.

Dredge 3 cups blueberries, fresh or frozen, in a bit of flour and fold in.

Grease and fill two 9 x 9 x 2-inch square pans, two 9 x 5 x 3-inch loaf pans, or two 9-inch tube pans. Bake in a preheated 350° oven for about 40 minutes or until done.

You can use any kind of topping for this: sprinkle with sugar, add Butter Streusel Topping (page 73), or frost with Sylvia's Fluffy Butter Cream Frosting (page 8) or Cream Cheese Frosting (page 45).

Sweet Cream Cake

 This is a nice cake to make when you have cream in the house and want to use it up.

In large bowl, beat until very thick, about 5 minutes:
   3 eggs
Beat in gradually:
   1 ^{1}/$_3$ cups sugar
Sift together:
   2 ^{1}/$_4$ cups sifted flour
   3 tsp. baking powder
   1 tsp. salt
Stir flour mixture into egg mixture alternately with:
   1 ^{1}/$_3$ cups rich cream
   1 ^{1}/$_2$ tsp. vanilla

Pour into greased and floured 9-inch tube pan and bake in preheated 350° oven for 45 to 55 minutes.

Frost with the frosting of your choice, or dust with confectioners' sugar and serve as a pound cake.

Chocolate Chip and Cherry Cake

 This recipe yields two loaves, and I've been making it for years. The cake is a favorite with my husband, Arnold. I always bake a few before Thanksgiving and Christmas.

Into a large bowl, sift:
   3 cups flour
   3 tsp. baking powder
   $^1/_2$ tsp. salt

Stir in (no need to chop):
   2 cups chocolate chips
   3 cups dates, cut in half
   2 cups cherries, maraschino or candied
   4 cups walnuts or pecans

In a large bowl, beat:
   6 eggs

Gradually beat in:
   2 cups sugar

Fold flour mixture into egg mixture.

Grease and line with wax paper two 9 x 5 x 3-inch loaf pans or two tube pans, then grease again. Add batter and bake in preheated 325° oven for 1 hour or until done. As soon as the cakes come out of the oven, pour $^1/_2$ cup of either brandy, bourbon, or rum over them. Leave in the pans until all liquor has been absorbed. If you think they need more, add to your taste. Next, these cakes should be double-wrapped in plastic wrap, put into freezer bags, and left to "ripen" in either the refrigerator or freezer for at least a week.

Strawberry Swirl Cake

Cream well:
  2 sticks butter or margarine
Beat in well:
  3 cups sugar
  $1/2$ tsp. salt
  1 tsp. almond flavoring
Add, one at a time, beating until well combined:
  6 large eggs
Beat in:
  3 cups flour
  $1/4$ tsp. baking soda
Alternately with:
  1 cup sour cream

Sprinkle bottom of a well greased 10-inch tube pan with chopped pecans. Layer the batter, putting about 1 cup of strawberry filling, below, in the middle. Before baking, you may sprinkle top with about $1/2$ cup pecan halves mixed with $1/2$ tsp. flour. Bake in a preheated 325° oven for 1 hour and 20 to 25 minutes.

Fruit filling:

  $2/3$ cup sugar
  $1/4$ cup cornstarch
  $3/4$ cup water
  2 cups fresh or frozen strawberries (or other fruit)
  1 Tbsp. lemon juice

Cook these together until transparent, and boil for about 5 minutes. Chill before layering with batter.

Note: Instead of making your own filling, you can use a half-can of Comstock strawberry filling or substitute other fruit fillings such as cherry, raspberry, etc.

Almond Glaze:

  $1 1/2$ cups confectioners' sugar
  $1/2$ tsp. almond flavoring
  hot water

Mix together until of glaze consistency, and drizzle over cake. Decorate top of cake with candied cherries and pecan halves.

Maple Pecan Cake

Delicious with penuche frosting (page 24 or page 54).

In large bowl, mix:
   2^1/3 cups flour
   1 cup sugar
   1 cup firmly packed brown sugar
   1 tsp. baking soda
   1 tsp. salt

Add and beat with mixer for 2 minutes:
   ^{2}/3 cup shortening
   1 cup buttermilk

Add and beat for 2 more minutes:
   3 eggs
   2 tsp. maple flavoring
   1 tsp. vanilla

Last, fold in:
   ^{2}/3 to 1 cup toasted chopped pecans.

Pour into well greased 13 x 9 x 2-inch pan or 10-inch tube pan and bake in preheated 350° oven for 45 to 55 minutes.

If you want a spice cake instead, leave out the maple flavoring and add:
   1^1/2 tsp. cinnamon
   ^{3}/4 tsp. nutmeg
   ^{3}/4 tsp. cloves

Maple Walnut Cake

 This recipe makes two large cakes.

Cream together well:
   1 cup shortening
   1 1/2 cups light brown sugar
   1 1/2 cups granulated sugar
Beat in thoroughly:
   4 extra-large eggs
Sift together:
   3 3/4 cups all-purpose flour
   2 tsp. baking soda
   1 tsp. salt
Add the dry ingredients alternately to the creamed mixture with:
   2 cups buttermilk
Add:
   3 tsp. maple flavoring
   1 tsp. vanilla
Lastly, fold in:
   2 cups chopped walnuts or pecans (toasted)

Grease and flour two 10-inch tube pans. Bake in 350° oven for 40 to 50 minutes or until done. The batter can also be divided to make layer cakes.

English Currant Cake

 This is similar to a pound cake and is very nice for afternoon tea. It's not too sweet. The recipe makes two large loaf cakes.

2 sticks butter or margarine	4 tsp. nutmeg
2 cups sugar	1 cup milk
4 extra-large eggs	2 cups dried currants
4 cups all-purpose flour	1 cup chopped nuts
4 tsp. baking powder	2 tsp. vanilla or lemon extract
1/2 tsp. salt	(optional)

Cream butter and sugar well. Add the eggs, one at a time, beating well. Sift the flour, baking powder, salt, and nutmeg together; add alternately to the creamed mixture with milk, beating until well blended. Fold in with a spoon the currants and nuts. (I always add some flavoring, either vanilla or lemon or a little of both.) Pour into two well greased 9 x 5 x 3-inch loaf pans, and bake in a preheated 350° oven for 40 to 50 minutes or until done. When cake has cooled, dust with confectioners' sugar.

German Prune Cake

 My old friend Vina Lind mailed me this recipe a number of years ago. She used it in place of fruitcake.

1 cup pitted, chopped prunes	$1/2$ tsp. allspice
$1/2$ cup raisins	$1 1/2$ cups sugar
1 cup chopped walnuts	1 cup oil
2 cups flour	1 cup buttermilk
1 tsp. baking soda	3 eggs
1 tsp. cinnamon	1 tsp. vanilla
1 tsp. nutmeg	1 tsp. salt

Grease and flour a bundt pan. Combine fruits and nuts with $1/2$ cup of the flour. Mix together all other ingredients and beat until creamy and smooth. Add floured fruits and nuts, folding in lightly. Pour batter into pan, and bake in preheated 325° oven for 45 minutes or until cake pulls away from sides of pan and springs back to the touch. This cake may be frozen successfully.

Make the glaze, below, while the cake is baking:

Buttermilk Glaze:

$1/2$ cup sugar
$1/2$ cup buttermilk
$1/2$ tsp. baking soda
$1/4$ cup butter

Combine all ingredients in a saucepan. Cook over medium heat, stirring until butter melts and mixture boils. Remove from heat. Pierce cake with meat fork. Slowly ladle mixture evenly over cake. After liquid is absorbed, turn cake out on rack and turn right-side up. Cool thoroughly.

Old-Time Raisin Cake

(No Eggs)

In a large kettle or Dutch oven, place:

- 2 heaping cups raisins
- 1 10-oz. box currants
- 2 sticks (1 cup) butter
- 1 1/2 tsp. salt
- 2 cups sugar
- 1 tsp. cinnamon
- 1/2 tsp. ground cloves
- 1 tsp. instant coffee
- 3 cups water

Bring to a boil, stirring occasionally. Boil for 15 minutes. Let cool.

Add:

- 20 oz. maraschino cherries, drained (optional)
- 2 tsp. baking soda
- 1 tsp. baking powder
- 2 tsp. vanilla
- 5 cups all-purpose flour

Stir into cooled mixture, mixing well. Grease two 9 x 5 x 3-inch loaf pans, and completely layer the bottoms with chopped pecans or walnuts. Divide batter between two pans.

Bake in a preheated 325° oven for 1 hour and 20 minutes. Be sure to test before removing from oven. Leave in pans for about 15 minutes, then turn out onto rack to cool.

This cake is delicious and keeps very well in a tin. It can be served as is or topped with Sylvia's Butter Cream Frosting, below.

Sylvia's Butter Cream Frosting:

- 6 Tbsp. butter
- 4 Tbsp. heavy cream or milk
- 1/8 tsp. salt

Put in saucepan or stainless steel bowl and heat until butter is melted. Remove from burner and add 1 tsp. vanilla and about 4 or 5 cups confectioners' sugar (more if needed) to make a spreadable icing. Add more cream if needed.

Pineapple Refrigerator Cake

 This was a favorite in our home when I was growing up; my mother made it often. It's luscious.

2 cups sifted cake flour
1 1/4 cups sugar
3 1/2 tsp. baking powder
1 tsp. salt
1 tsp. grated lemon rind

1/2 cup shortening
1 cup less 2 Tbsp. canned
 pineapple juice
1 tsp. vanilla
3 egg whites, unbeaten

Sift all dry ingredients into mixing bowl; add lemon rind. Drop in shortening, add pineapple juice and vanilla, and beat for 2 minutes with mixer set at low speed. Add egg whites, and beat 2 more minutes at low speed. Bake in two square 8 x 8 x 2-inch greased pans in preheated 360° oven 25 to 30 minutes. Remove from oven when done, and allow to cool. Chill layers and split in half. Spread layers with pineapple filling, below, and sweetened whipped cream, stack them, and cover top with more whipped cream.

Pineapple Filling:

3/4 cup sugar
2 1/2 Tbsp. cornstarch
1/8 tsp. salt
1/4 cup lemon juice

grated rind of 1 lemon
3 egg yolks, beaten slightly
1/2 cup canned pineapple juice
2 Tbsp. butter

Mix sugar, cornstarch, and salt in top of double boiler. Add lemon juice and rind; mix well. Add egg yolks, pineapple juice, and butter; blend thoroughly. Place over boiling water and cook until smooth and thick, stirring constantly (about 15 minutes).

After applying filling and whipped cream, store cake in refrigerator for several hours before serving. Remove and cut into slices about 1-inch thick. Serve immediately.

Banana Cake with
Peanut Butter Frosting

This one was a favorite when our sons were growing up.

1/2 cup shortening
1/2 tsp. salt
1 1/2 cups sugar
2 eggs, well beaten
1 tsp. vanilla
1 tsp. baking soda
3/4 cups buttermilk or sour milk
2 cups flour
1 cup banana pulp (two large bananas)
1 cup chopped nuts

Cream shortening, salt, and sugar; blend well. Add eggs and vanilla. Dissolve baking soda in sour milk, and add to mixture. Add flour, and blend in. Add banana pulp and nut meats. Pour batter into a well greased 8 x 8 x 2-inch or 9 x 9 x 2-inch pan Bake in a preheated 350° oven for 45 to 50 minutes.

Peanut Butter Frosting:

2 Tbsp. butter or margarine
1/4 cup hot water
2 cups confectioners' sugar
1/4 cup peanut butter
1 tsp. vanilla

Heat butter and water to boiling point. Pour over sugar. Stir in peanut butter. Beat until smooth and creamy. Spread quickly over top.

Apple Bundt Cake

Beat together well:
    1 cup oil
    1 1/3 cups sugar
    1 tsp. vanilla
    1 tsp. salt
    1 tsp. cinnamon
Add, one at a time:
    3 eggs
Mix together and add:
    2 cups flour
    1 tsp. baking soda
    2 heaping cups chopped apples

Sprinkle the bottom of a well-greased bundt pan or 10-inch tube pan with pecan halves. Cover with batter, and sprinkle with pecan halves and a mixture of cinnamon and sugar. Bake in a preheated 350° oven for about 50 minutes or until done.

Fruit and Nut Delight

    1 1/2 cups flour
    1 tsp. baking powder
    1/2 tsp. salt
    1 1/2 cups sugar
    1 large can crushed pineapple, drained
    2 (16 oz.) jars maraschino cherries (drained) or candied cherries
    5 cups nuts (pecans, brazil nuts, walnuts, or almonds)
    1 pkg. (16 oz.) light raisins
    1 or 2 more cups candied pineapple
    6 eggs
    1/3 cup pineapple juice or dark rum

Combine first nine ingredients. Beat eggs well, and add the rum or pineapple juice. Blend this well with the first mixture.

Transfer batter into three 8 1/2 x 4 1/2 x 2 1/2-inch pans. Bake in a preheated 300° oven for 1 1/2 hours.

Note: Rum may be poured over the cakes when they come out of the oven. This will keep them moist.

Cranberry Butter and
Sour Cream Cake

 This was a great favorite among customers from all over the country.

1 1/2 sticks of butter or margarine
1 cup sugar
2 eggs
2 cups flour
1 tsp. baking powder
1 tsp. baking soda
1/2 tsp. salt
1 cup sour cream
1 tsp. almond extract (or more)
1 cup whole cranberry sauce
pecan halves for garnish

Cream butter or margarine well, and slowly add sugar, beating well. Add eggs, one at a time; cream well. Sift flour, baking powder, baking soda, and salt together; add to creamed mixture alternately with a combination of sour cream and almond extract.

Prepare a 9-inch tube pan by greasing and flouring both the bottom and the center tube. Spoon half of the batter into the pan; cover this with cranberry sauce, then put in the other half of the batter. With a table knife, swirl this around to lightly blend. Sprinkle the top with pecan halves.

Bake in preheated 350° oven for 45 to 50 minutes.

Glaze for Cranberry Cake:

1 to 1 1/2 cups confectioners' sugar
1/2 tsp. almond flavoring
hot water

Mix together until of glaze consistency, and drizzle over top of cake. Decorate top with candied cherry halves and pecan halves.

Soft Molasses Gingerbread

 This gingerbread is very moist and delicious. It's especially good when served warm with whipped cream or vanilla ice cream.

Sift into mixing bowl:

$2^1/_2$ level cups all-purpose flour

1 tsp. salt

1 tsp. baking soda

1 tsp. baking powder

1 tsp. ginger

1 tsp. cinnamon

$^1/_2$ cup sugar

Add:

$^1/_2$ cup melted shortening or butter

1 egg, well beaten

1 cup molasses

Last, add:

1 cup boiling water or coffee

Pour batter into a greased 9 x 9 x 2-inch or 13 x 9 x 2-inch baking pan. Bake in a preheated 375° oven for about 25 minutes.

Cream Cheese Pound Cake

 This is a new pound cake recipe to me. It is a little drier in texture than the ones I'm used to, but it is worth trying— especially at holiday time. I have made a swirl cake from this recipe by layering a fruit filling in the middle, then swirling the batter with a knife before baking. It's very nice in a bundt pan.

Cream together well:
   1 cup butter
   1 (8 oz.) pkg. cream cheese

Add:
   1 1/2 cups sugar
   4 eggs, beating in one at a time
   1 1/2 tsp. vanilla

Stir together:
   2 1/4 cups cake flour
   1 1/2 tsp. baking powder
   1/2 tsp. salt
Add these dry ingredients to the creamed mixture just until well mixed.

Fold in last:
   3/4 cup well drained maraschino cherries
   1 cup pecans, divided

Grease well a 10-inch tube pan, and sprinkle with 1/2 cup nuts. Pour batter into prepared pan. Bake in preheated 325° oven for about 70 minutes. Cool cake in pan for 5 minutes on wire rack before removing. Cool thoroughly.

   Make a glaze with 1 1/2 Tbsp. milk and 1 1/2 cups confectioners' sugar; drizzle this over the top of cake. Garnish top with cherries and pecans if desired. (Makes 12 to 16 servings.)

The Best Lemon Butter
Pound Cake

 This is undoubtedly one of the most popular cakes that ever came out of my shop! I shipped them all over the United States and got nothing but rave reports. This recipe is well worth your trouble and expense. I'm sure it will become your favorite, also.

Note: Ingredients should be room temperature, unless you are baking in hot weather.

In large bowl, beat with mixer until light and fluffy:
   2 sticks butter
   $^1/_2$ cup shortening
   $2^2/_3$ cups sugar
   3 cups all-purpose flour
   1 tsp. salt
   1 cup milk

Add to this and beat until blended:
   1 tsp. baking powder
   $2^1/_2$ Tbsp. lemon extract

Add:
   5 eggs, one at a time
Beat until completely blended.

Butter and line with chopped pecans a 10-inch tube pan or two 9 x 5 x 3-inch loaf pans. Add batter and bake in a preheated 325° oven for 1 hour and 20 minutes or until done. For best results, test for doneness with metal cake tester or toothpick. As soon as cake comes out of the oven, prick the top all over with a meat fork and loosen cake from pan sides and tube with a straight table knife.

Ladle over cake a mixture of:
   8 oz. thawed, concentrated lemonade
   1 cup (or more) sugar

Let this soak in, then sprinkle top lightly with sugar. Turn out onto cake rack with the top of cake right-side up. Sprinkle top with more sugar to make a crunchy texture.

Chocolate Butter Pound Cake

 This was a big favorite among my shop and mail-order customers. It is very rich and chocolaty. I always put a thin chocolate glaze on top.

Cream well:
   2 sticks butter
   $1/2$ cup shortening
   3 cups sugar
   2 tsp. vanilla
   2 tsp. brandy (optional)
   $1/4$ tsp. salt
Add, one at a time:
   5 eggs
Beat until well blended.

Sift together:
   3 cups flour
   1 tsp. baking powder
   $3/4$ cup unsweetened cocoa
Add these dry ingredients to the creamed mixture alternately with:
   $1\,1/4$ cups milk
Beat well.

Fold in:
   1 cup chopped pecans or walnuts

Pour batter into a well greased 10-inch tube pan or two 9 x 5 x 3-inch loaf pans. Bake in a preheated 325° oven for about 1 hour and 20 minutes. Be sure to test for doneness with a cake tester.

Glaze:

   $1\,1/2$ squares unsweetened baking chocolate
   2 Tbsp. butter
   confectioners' sugar
   1 tsp. vanilla

In a saucepan, melt baking chocolate with butter. Remove from burner; add enough confectioners' sugar and hot water to make glaze thin enough to drizzle on cake, adding 1 tsp. vanilla last.

Cream Cheese
and
Butter Pound Cake

Cream well:
  2 sticks butter
  $1/2$ cup Crisco shortening
  1 block (8 oz.) cream cheese
  $1/2$ tsp. salt

Slowly add:
  3 cups sugar
  1 Tbsp. pure vanilla
Cream this all very well.

Add:
  6 eggs, 2 at a time, alternately with 3 cups of flour
Beating well after each addition.

Fold in:
  $1^{1}/2$ cups toasted pecans, if desired.

Grease well and line a 10-inch tube pan with chopped pecans. Pour in batter, and bake in a preheated 325° oven for 1 hour and 30 minutes or until done. Be sure to test. This cake will fill the tube pan to the top when baked. (It can also be divided into two large loaf pans.) When cool, sift all over with confectioners' sugar.

Note: Try substituting 2 Tbsp. lemon flavoring in place of the vanilla in the cake and pouring this batter into two 13 x 9 x 2-inch pans, each well buttered and sprinkled with chopped nuts. Bake these in a 350° oven for about 40 minutes. Be sure to test for doneness. When you remove cakes from oven, prick all over with a meat fork; pour lemon glaze (thawed lemonade concentrate mixed with sugar so it is runny) all over the cakes. Don't use too much, as these have to be cut in squares and served as bars. Sprinkle all over with some granulated sugar to make a crunchy topping.

Mother Adams's Marble Pound Cake

 My mother used to love to make this cake. The recipe appeared in Yankee *magazine in 1995 and in the 1997* Yankee *calendar.*

In large mixing bowl, place:

2³/₄ cups flour

2¹/₄ tsp. baking powder

1 tsp. salt

1³/₄ cups sugar

Add and beat for 2 minutes:

³/₄ cup milk

2 sticks butter or margarine

1¹/₂ tsp. vanilla

Add and beat for 2 more minutes:

4 eggs

Add to one half of batter:

1 cup chocolate bits, melted

Pour the light half of the batter into a greased 10-inch tube pan, and cover with the chocolate half. Draw a knife through to swirl layers slightly. Bake in a preheated 350° oven for 55 to 65 minutes or until done.

Note: For the chocolate part, you can also use 1 square unsweetened chocolate melted with 1 Tbsp. shortening, or ³/₄ cup chocolate syrup with ¹/₄ tsp. baking soda mixed in.

Frosting:

In medium size saucepan, place:

2 squares unsweetened chocolate

2 Tbsp. butter

1 Tbsp. corn syrup

Melt these together, stirring constantly to keep from sticking. Remove from burner.

Add:

1¹/₂ to 2 cups confectioners' sugar

2 to 3 Tbsp. hot water or coffee

1 tsp. vanilla

Beat together until of spreading consistency. Cover top of cake, and circle all around with pecan halves.

Shirley Watkins' Pound Cake

$1/2$ lb. butter (2 sticks)
$1/2$ cup shortening
3 cups sugar
5 eggs
1 cup milk
3 cups flour

$1/4$ tsp. mace
$1/2$ tsp. baking powder
1 tsp. salt
$1/2$ tsp. lemon extract
1 tsp. vanilla

Cream butter and shortening with sugar. Add eggs, one at a time, beating after each. Blend in milk. Add flour, mace, baking powder, salt, and lemon and vanilla flavorings.

Place in greased 10-inch tube pan. Put into a cold oven. Bake at 325° about $1 1/2$ to $1 3/4$ hours. Cool 10 to 15 minutes before removing from pan.

This cake is nice with lemon glaze dribbled over the top and down the sides and with grated lemon zest on top.

Butter Pound Cake with Sour Cream

2 sticks butter
3 cups sugar
6 large eggs
3 cups all purpose flour

$1/2$ tsp. salt
$1/4$ tsp. baking soda
2 tsp. pure vanilla
1 cup sour cream

Cream the butter and sugar well. Add 2 eggs and beat; add 1 cup flour. Continue to alternate eggs and flour, and beat after each addition. (Be sure to add the salt and baking soda with the flour.) Add vanilla, and mix in well. Fold in sour cream until all is well combined. Pour this into a greased and floured 10-inch tube pan. Place pan in a cold oven and set to 325°. Do not open oven for 1 hour. Bake cake for 1 hour and about 30 minutes.

Note: During the holidays, I add 1 cup candied cherries, 1 cup nuts, 1 cup candied pineapple, all lightly floured and folded in last. And, I sometimes divide the batter in two, transferring it to well buttered 9 x 5 x 3-inch loaf pans. I dust the tops with confectioners' sugar after the cakes have cooled.

Sour Cream Pound Cake
#1

1 1/2 sticks butter
2 cups sugar
4 eggs
1 tsp. vanilla
1/4 tsp. almond extract

1/4 tsp. lemon extract
1 tsp. grated lemon rind
2 1/4 cups flour
1/8 tsp. baking soda
3/4 cup sour cream

Cream together the butter and sugar; add the eggs, one at a time, mixing in well. Add flavorings and rind. Combine flour and baking soda; add alternately with the sour cream to the creamed mixture.

Pour into a greased and floured bundt pan. Bake in a preheated 325 ° oven for 1 hour and 5 minutes or until done.

Sour Cream Pound Cake
#2

2 sticks butter
1/2 cup shortening
3 cups sugar
1/2 tsp. salt
5 eggs
3 cups flour

1/2 tsp. baking powder
1 cup sour cream
1/4 cup milk
2 tsp. lemon extract
1 tsp. vanilla
chopped pecans for garnish

Cream butter, shortening, sugar, and salt together; beat well. Add eggs, one at a time, beating well. Mix flour and baking powder together; add to the creamed mixture alternately with sour cream/milk mixture. Beat in lemon and vanilla extracts.

Place batter in large tube pan that has been well greased and sprinkled with chopped pecans. Bake in a preheated 325° oven for 1 1/2 hours. Do not open oven door during the first hour of baking.

Icing:

1 stick butter, softened
1 (3 oz.) pkg. cream cheese, softened
1 lb. confectioners' sugar
3 to 4 Tbsp. lemon juice

Beat together well.

Blueberry Sour Cream Pound Cake

 Delicious and very popular with my customers.

1 cup butter	3 cups flour
2 cups sugar	$^1/_2$ tsp. baking powder
1 tsp. vanilla	$^1/_4$ tsp. baking soda
$^1/_2$ tsp. salt	1 cup sour cream
6 eggs	4 cups blueberries (fresh or frozen)

Cream together for six minutes butter, sugar, vanilla, and salt. Add the eggs one at a time, blending well after each addition. To this mixture, add flour, baking powder, and baking soda sifted together, blending alternately with sour cream. Fold in blueberries.

This cake can be baked at 325° in one 10-inch tube pan for 1 hour and 25 minutes or two 9-inch tube pans for about 1 hour. In both cases, it's good with Butter Streusel Topping (page 73). Or, you can use two $9^1/_2$ x 5 x 3-inch loaf pans (bake for 45 to 60 minutes) or two 13 x 9 x 2-inch oblong pans (bake 45 to 50 minutes). The sheet cakes are good when spread with Cream Cheese Frosting, below, and topped with chopped nuts. Cut in squares as you would for bar cookies.

Cream Cheese Frosting:

Cream well:
    1 (8-oz.) pkg. cream cheese, softened
    1 stick butter, softened

Add:
    1 tsp. vanilla
    3 to 4 cups confectioners' sugar

Add milk or cream if needed. This amount will frost two 13 x 9 x 2-inch cakes. As a final touch, sprinkle the tops of the frosted cakes with chopped walnuts.

Orange Pound Cake

2 sticks butter
1/2 cup shortening
1/2 tsp. salt
3 cups sugar
5 large eggs

1 Tbsp. orange extract
3 cups flour
1 tsp. baking powder
1 cup milk

Cream together the butter, shortening, salt, and sugar until fluffy. Add the eggs one at a time, blending well after each addition. Add the orange extract. Mix together the flour and baking powder. Add this to the creamed mixture alternately with the milk, mixing in well.

Grease and flour a 10-inch tube pan or two 9 x 5 x 3-inch loaf pans. Bake in a preheated 325° oven for about 70 minutes or until done.

Orange Glaze:

Combine in a saucepan:
    1 cup confectioners' sugar
    1/4 cup orange juice
    1/4 tsp. grated rind

Simmer on low heat while cake is baking. Prick top of cake with meat fork when it comes out of the oven, and pour glaze over the top.

Brown Sugar Pound Cake

1 lb. brown sugar (2 1/4 cups)
3/4 cup white sugar
3/4 cup shortening
3/4 cup butter
5 large eggs
3 cups flour

1 tsp. salt
1 tsp. baking powder
1 cup milk
1 1/2 tsp. vanilla
1 cup chopped nuts

Cream together well sugars, shortening, and butter. Add eggs, one at a time, blending each well. Mix flour, salt, and baking powder; add to creamed mixture alternately with milk and vanilla. Beat until well blended. Fold in the chopped nuts last. Pour into well greased and floured 10-inch tube pan, and bake in a preheated 325° oven for 1 hour and 20 minutes or until done. May be frosted with Penuche Frosting (page 54) or dusted all over with confectioners' sugar.

Rum Pound Cake with
Rum Butter Glaze

1 cup butter
$^1/_2$ cup shortening
2$^1/_2$ cups sugar
5 eggs
3$^1/_4$ cups flour

$^1/_2$ tsp. baking powder
$^1/_2$ tsp. salt
1 cup milk
1 Tbsp. light or dark rum

Thoroughly cream the butter, shortening, and sugar. Add the eggs, one at a time, beating well. Mix the flour, baking powder, and salt; add alternately to the creamed mixture with the milk and the rum. Mix well. Cover the bottom of a well greased 10-inch tube pan with 1 cup chopped pecans, and pour batter over it. Bake in a preheated 325° oven for 1 hour, then turn the temperature to 300° for about 20 minutes or until done. Prick top of cake with a meat fork, and pour the glaze of your choice over the top.

Glaze #1:

Combine and bring to a boil:
   1 cup brown sugar
   $^1/_3$ cup water
   $^1/_2$ stick butter
Remove from heat, add:
   2 tsp. rum or rum flavoring
Pour over hot cake.

Glaze #2 (Sylvia's choice):

   1 stick butter
   $^1/_4$ cup water
   1 cup sugar
   $^1/_2$ cup Bacardi dark rum

Melt butter in saucepan; stir in water and sugar. Boil 5 minutes, stirring constantly. Remove from heat. Stir in rum. Pour over cake.

Note: Bourbon whiskey may be substituted for the rum in the cake and glaze.

Frostings, Glazes, & Fillings

Fudge Frosting

 This recipe will frost one large cake. Be sure to work quickly—it will harden very fast!

Combine in saucepan:
 3 cups sugar
 1 cup water
 2 Tbsp. corn syrup
 2 Tbsp. butter
 4 squares unsweetened chocolate, cut up
Heat and stir until chocolate melts.

Now cook, without stirring, to the soft-ball stage (234°), keeping covered for the first 3 minutes. Remove from heat. Let stand until cool. Add 1 $^1/_2$ tsp. vanilla, and beat until thick enough to hold shape.

Note: When fudge-type frostings become too thick to spread, add a little cream as needed. When too thin, add sifted confectioners' sugar.

My Mother's Chocolate-Mocha Frosting

1 lb. confectioners' sugar
$^1/_2$ cup cocoa
$^1/_8$ tsp. salt

1 tsp. vanilla
$^1/_3$ cup strong coffee
2 Tbsp. melted butter

Mix all ingredients and beat well. Add the melted butter last—just before frosting cake. This recipe will cover the tops and sides of two 9-inch layers.

Quick Fudge Frosting

$1/2$ cup sugar
3 Tbsp. unsweetened cocoa or 2 squares unsweetened chocolate
4 Tbsp. butter or margarine
$1/3$ cup milk
2 Tbsp. light corn syrup
$1/8$ tsp. salt
$1 1/2$ or 2 cups confectioners' sugar
1 tsp. vanilla

Mix sugar and cocoa in medium-size saucepan. Add the butter, milk, corn syrup, and salt. On low heat, bring to a boil, stirring frequently. Boil for 2 minutes, stirring occasionally. Cool slightly. Beat in confectioners' sugar and vanilla. Use enough sugar to make a soft, spreadable frosting. Will frost the top of an 8- or 9-inch square or round cake. This frosting can be sprinkled with chopped nuts.

Cocoa Fudge Frosting

$1/2$ cup unsweetened cocoa
4 cups confectioners' sugar
5 Tbsp. milk
$1/2$ cup butter or margarine
1 tsp. vanilla

Combine cocoa, 1 cup of confectioners' sugar, milk, and butter in saucepan. Stir over medium heat just to boiling point. Remove from heat. Pour into mixing bowl. Gradually add remaining confectioners' sugar, beating at medium-low speed of electric mixer. Blend in vanilla. Continue beating until frosting is of spreading consistency. Add more sugar if needed.

Sylvia's Creamy Mocha Frosting

 For many years, this has been a favorite frosting for my chocolate fudge cakes. The recipe will generously cover a large layer cake. Spread it nice and thick, as it is not too sweet and is always a real favorite! I always cover the top of the frosting with chocolate sprills.

Beat in large mixing bowl:
   1 egg (cold)
   1 cup shortening (I use Crisco)
   1 stick butter, softened
   $^1/_8$ tsp. salt
The result should look like very creamy mayonnaise.

Add:
   4 squares melted unsweetened chocolate, slightly cooled
Continue beating until all one color.

Have ready:
   about $^3/_4$ cup very hot, strong coffee
Add to creamy mixture:
   2 lb.-plus confectioners' sugar
   2 tsp. vanilla
   about $^1/_4$ cup coffee, or more if needed (see above)

Beat on low speed until all blended; if additional liquid is needed, add more coffee. Now beat on medium speed for 10 minutes or until frosting has a creamy, spreading consistency. Add more confectioners' sugar or coffee as required.

Note: This amount will also generously frost the tops of two square 9 x 9 x 2-inch cakes or two 9-inch tube-pan cakes.

   If you are concerned about using raw eggs, this frosting can be made without them, but it isn't quite as good.

Chocolate Mocha Frosting

$3/4$ cup shortening
1 tsp. vanilla
$1/2$ tsp. salt
$1/2$ cup cocoa
$4 1/2$ cups confectioners' sugar
$1/2$ cup strong brewed coffee
        (or 1 Tbsp. instant coffee dissolved in $1/2$ cup hot water)

Cream shortening, vanilla, salt, and cocoa. Add sugar and coffee alternately to creamed mixture, beating until smooth. The recipe will frost and fill a 9-inch layer cake.

Chocolate Butter Frosting

 This is just the right amount to completely frost a 9-inch layer cake.

$2/3$ cup butter or margarine, softened
4 squares melted, unsweetened chocolate
        (or $2/3$ cup unsweetened cocoa)
4 cups confectioners' sugar (or more)
3 tsp. vanilla
4 Tbsp. milk (or more)

Mix thoroughly the butter and cooled chocolate. Blend in the sugar; stir in the vanilla and milk; beat until frosting is smooth and of spreading consistency.

Chocolate Cream Cheese Frosting

3 squares unsweetened chocolate
$1/4$ cup butter or margarine
1 (8 oz.) pkg. softened cream cheese
3 cups confectioners' sugar, divided
1 Tbsp. plus 1 tsp. whipping cream
$1/8$ tsp. salt
$1/2$ tsp. vanilla

Melt chocolate in a heavy saucepan over low heat, stirring constantly; cool. Cream the butter and the cream cheese; add 1 cup confectioners' sugar, melted chocolate, cream, salt, and vanilla, beating well. Add remaining 2 cups confectioners' sugar; beat until of spreading consistency.

Note: This recipe will frost a layer cake.

Chocolate Glaze

 This is a nice glaze to top a pound cake or a small pan of squares.

Combine in saucepan:
  3 Tbsp. water
  $^{1}/_{8}$ tsp. salt
  2 Tbsp. butter
Bring to a full boil, remove from heat.

Immediately stir in:
  3 Tbsp. unsweetened cocoa
Beat in until smooth:
  1 cup confectioners' sugar
  $^{1}/_{2}$ tsp. vanilla
Cool slightly.

Butter Glaze for Applesauce Cake

  4 Tbsp. melted butter
  1-plus cups confectioners' sugar
  $^{1}/_{2}$ tsp. lemon flavoring
  $^{1}/_{4}$ tsp. orange flavoring
  2 Tbsp. boiling water

Mix together until of glaze consistency. Drizzle over top of cake and decorate with walnut halves and candied cherries.

Butter Frosting

Cook, stirring, until thick:
    3 Tbsp. flour
    1 cup water
Cool.

Cream together:
    1 cup confectioners' sugar
    1 cup (2 sticks) butter or margarine
    1 tsp. vanilla
Cream together until sugar is dissolved.

Add the cooled, flour mixture to this one, and blend together well. Then beat with mixer until thick, about 10 minutes.

Quick Caramel Frosting

 This is delicious on a spice cake, apple cake, or chocolate cake, as well as a plain vanilla cake.

    $1/2$ cup butter (no substitutes)
    1 cup firmly packed brown sugar
    $1/4$ cup milk
    $1^3/4$ to $2^1/2$ cups confectioners' sugar

Melt butter in saucepan; add brown sugar. Heat over low heat for 2 minutes, stirring until mixture comes to a boil. Add milk and boil again, stirring constantly. Remove from heat; cool. Gradually add confectioners' sugar, beating well after each addition, until of spreading consistency.

Penuche Frosting

    $1^1/2$ cups brown sugar
    1 stick butter
    $1/4$ tsp. salt
    $1/4$ cup milk
    $1^1/2$ cups confectioners' sugar

Combine brown sugar, butter, and salt in saucepan; bring to a boil. Add milk, boil slowly 3 minutes, and cool. Add confectioners' sugar, and beat until thick enough to spread, adding more sugar if needed.

Satiny Beige Frosting

1 cup brown sugar
4 Tbsp. water
$^1/_2$ cup light corn syrup
4 egg whites, room temperature
1 tsp. vanilla

Mix brown sugar, water, and syrup in saucepan; cover and bring to a rolling boil. Remove cover and cook to 242° or until syrup spins a 6- to 8-inch thread. Just before syrup is ready, beat egg whites until stiff enough to hold a point. Continue beating while pouring hot syrup very slowly in a thin stream into egg whites. Beat until frosting holds peaks. Blend in vanilla.

Note: This frosting is delicious on my mother's spice cake in layers with crushed walnuts sprinkled on the top.

White Mountain Frosting

My mother gave me this recipe many, many years ago. She almost always frosted layer cakes with either this icing, seven-minute frosting, or Satiny Beige Frosting (above).

$^1/_2$ cup sugar
2 Tbsp. water
$^1/_4$ cup light corn syrup
2 egg whites ($^1/_4$ cup)
1 tsp. vanilla

Mix sugar, water, and syrup in saucepan; cover and bring to a rolling boil. Remove cover and cook to 242° or until syrup spins a 6- to 8-inch thread. Just before syrup is ready, beat egg whites until stiff enough to hold a point. Continue beating while pouring hot syrup very slowly in thin stream into egg whites. Beat until frosting holds peaks. Blend in vanilla.

Note: To fully frost a large layer cake, this recipe should be doubled.

Brandy Icing

Add 1 Tbsp. brandy or bourbon and $^1/_2$ tsp. vanilla to 1 cup confectioners' sugar. Add 1 to 2 Tbsp. milk and blend until icing is of drizzling consistency, adding more sugar if needed. Garnish cake with candied fruit, if desired.

Lemon Filling

 This is wonderful for a Silver White Cake (page 14), which is then frosted with whipped cream. Just right for a party!

$^3/_4$ cup sugar
3 Tbsp. cornstarch
$^1/_4$ tsp. salt
$^3/_4$ cup water
1 tsp. grated lemon peel
1 Tbsp. butter
$^1/_3$ cup lemon juice
4 drops yellow food coloring (optional)

Mix sugar, cornstarch, and salt in saucepan. Stir in water gradually. Cook, stirring constantly, until mixture thickens and boils. Boil and stir 1 minute. Remove from heat; add lemon peel and butter. Stir in lemon juice and food coloring. Cool. If filling is too soft, refrigerate until set.

Note: I don't use the food coloring.

Lemon Custard Filling

Beat until thick and lemon-colored:
    4 egg yolks
Gradually beat in:
    $^1/_2$ cup sugar
Blend in:
    4 Tbsp. lemon juice
    2 Tbsp. grated lemon rind

Cook over hot water, stirring constantly, until thick (5 to 8 minutes.) Cool before using.

Cooked Fruit Filling

$^2/_3$ cup sugar
$^1/_4$ cup cornstarch
$^3/_4$ cup water
2 cups fresh or frozen fruit
1 Tbsp. fresh lemon juice
2 Tbsp. butter

Combine all ingredients in a saucepan, and cook until transparent—about 5 to 7 minutes.

If you want to make a tart or pie, add 2 to 3 cups more fruit to the mixture after you've cooked the first part. Pour filling into a 9- or 10-inch baked crust. Serve with whipped cream.

Note: Use either strawberries, raspberries, blueberries, or a combination.

Date Nut Filling

$1^1/_2$ cups chopped dates
1 cup water
$^1/_3$ cup sugar
$^1/_4$ tsp. salt
$^1/_4$ cup chopped walnuts

Combine chopped dates, water, sugar, and salt in saucepan; bring to boiling. Cook and stir over low heat about 4 minutes or until thick. Remove from heat; cool to room temperature. Fold in chopped walnuts. Makes about $1^1/_2$ cups filling.

This is very nice for the filling in date nut bars. Use the recipe for Layered Oatmeal Bars (page 127).

Muffins, Pancakes, & Coffee Cakes

Blueberry Muffins

 These are so delicious!

2 heaping cups flour	$1/8$ tsp. cinnamon
1 tsp. salt	2 large eggs
$3/4$ cup sugar	$1/2$ cup oil or melted butter
3 tsp. baking powder	1 cup milk
3 cups blueberries	1 tsp. vanilla

In a large bowl, mix flour, salt, sugar, baking powder, blueberries, and cinnamon. In another bowl, mix together with a fork: eggs, oil or melted butter, milk, and vanilla. Add this all at once to the first mixture, and stir just until moistened. Do not beat.

This will make a dozen large muffins, which I sprinkle with sugar before baking. I use liners in my muffin tin, filling each one about two-thirds of the way with batter. Bake in a preheated 375° to 400° oven for about 20 to 25 minutes.

Note: You can substitute either raspberries or blackberries for the blueberries, or you can combine the three. Less sugar may be used if sugar intake is a concern.

Buttermilk Blueberry Muffins

2 1/2 cups flour
2 1/2 tsp. baking powder
1 cup sugar
1/4 tsp. salt

1 cup buttermilk
2 eggs, beaten
1 stick butter, melted
1 1/2 cups blueberries (I use more)

Mix dry ingredients together in large bowl; in another bowl, blend buttermilk, eggs, and butter with a fork, and add all at once to first mixture, stirring only to moisten. Fold in blueberries, and spoon batter into greased or lined muffin tins, filling two-thirds full. Bake in a preheated 400° oven for 20 minutes. Makes twelve muffins.

Gingerbread Muffins

 Makes three dozen, and batter keeps in refrigerator for two weeks.

1 cup shortening
1 cup sugar
1 cup molasses
4 eggs
2 tsp. baking soda
1 cup buttermilk

4 cups flour
1 Tbsp. plus 1 tsp. ground ginger
1 tsp. allspice
1/2 tsp. nutmeg
1/2 cup raisins
1/2 cup pecans

Cream shortening; gradually add sugar, beating with electric mixer at medium speed until light and fluffy. Add molasses. Add eggs, one at a time, beating well after each addition. Dissolve baking soda in buttermilk. Combine flour and spices; add to creamed mixture alternately with buttermilk, beating after each addition. Stir in raisins and pecans, if desired. Cover batter and store in refrigerator.

When ready to bake, spoon batter into greased or lined muffin pans, filling two-thirds full. Bake in preheated 350° oven for 20 minutes or until done.

Priscilla's Banana Pancakes

 These are yummy!

Sift together:
   1 1/2 cups flour
   3 tsp. baking powder
   3/4 tsp. salt
   1 Tbsp. sugar
Mix together:
   1 egg, well beaten
   1 1/3 cups milk
   3 Tbsp. melted butter

Add this to the dry ingredients, and stir to mix well.

Last, fold in:
   1 cup diced bananas.

Cook on hot griddle.

Hawaiian Pancake

Serves two people.

   1/2 cup flour
   1/2 cup milk
   2 eggs, beaten
   1/8 tsp. nutmeg
   1/2 stick butter or margarine, melted
   2 Tbsp. confectioners' sugar
   juice of two lemons

Combine flour, milk, eggs, and nutmeg. Mix well. Place in greased round cake pan. Pour melted butter on top. Bake in preheated oven at 425° for 15 to 20 minutes. Sprinkle with powdered sugar and lemon juice. Serve right away.

Cinnamon Swirl Coffee Cake

 When I first started baking to sell, it was just yeast breads and sweet breads. Then I started making coffee cakes. This is one of my favorites, and I think it is Essie Dondis's recipe. It was always very popular!

Cake:

> 1/2 cup butter or margarine
> 1 cup sugar
> 2 eggs
> 1 tsp. vanilla
> 2 cups all-purpose flour
> 1 tsp. baking powder
> 1 tsp. baking soda
> 1/4 tsp. salt
> 1 cup sour cream

Topping:

> 1/2 cup chopped nuts
> 1 tsp. cinnamon
> 1/4 cup sugar

Cream together butter and sugar. Add eggs, one at a time; add vanilla and beat well. Sift flour, baking soda, baking powder, and salt; add these to the creamed mixture alternately with sour cream.

Pour half of batter into a greased 9-inch or 10-inch tube pan. Sprinkle half of topping over batter in the pan. Add rest of batter, spreading evenly, and sprinkle rest of topping on top. Bake in a preheated 350° oven for 35 to 45 minutes.

Note: This coffee cake is also good with a tart lemon or orange glaze dribbled over the top. I used to do this during Christmas and would decorate the cake with candied cherry halves.

Glaze:

> 1 cup confectioners' sugar
> 1 to 2 Tbsp. butter, melted
> lemon or orange juice

Mix together to make a glaze thin enough for drizzling.

Cinnamon-Laced Sour Cream Cake

Combine and set aside:

$^1/_2$ cup chopped pecans

2 Tbsp. sugar

1 tsp. cinnamon

Cake:

2 sticks butter or margarine

2 cups sugar

2 eggs

2 cups flour

1 tsp. baking powder

$^1/_8$ tsp. salt

1 tsp. vanilla

1 cup (8 oz.) sour cream

Cream butter; gradually add 2 cups sugar, and beat well with mixer at medium speed. Add eggs, one at a time, beating after each addition. Combine flour, baking powder, and salt; add to creamed mixture, mixing just until blended. Stir in vanilla. Gently fold sour cream into batter.

Pour half of batter into a greased and floured 10-inch bundt pan. Sprinkle half of pecan mixture over batter. Repeat procedure. Bake in pre-heated 350° oven for 45 to 55 minutes. Sift confectioners' sugar over top.

Blueberry Coffee Cake

 This one is a little different but really worth trying. I baked one for a picnic and used raspberries instead of blueberries—it was a big hit! The results are equally as good with blueberries, though.

Topping:

 ¹/₄ cup flour
 ¹/₃ cup brown sugar
 1 tsp. cinnamon
 ¹/₄ cup butter
 ¹/₂ cup chopped nuts

Stir flour, brown sugar, cinnamon, and butter with fork until mixture is crumbly. Stir in nuts. Set aside.

Cake:

 3 cups flour
 1 cup sugar
 4 tsp. baking powder
 1 tsp. salt
 3 eggs, slightly beaten
 ¹/₂ cup sour cream
 ²/₃ cup milk
 ¹/₂ cup butter, melted
 1 ¹/₂ tsp. vanilla
 2 cups blueberries or raspberries
 1 (8 oz.) pkg. cream cheese, cut in ¹/₂-inch cubes

In a large bowl, mix dry ingredients, blending well with a wooden spoon. The blueberries and cream cheese cubes may be folded in now.

In another bowl, beat the eggs with a fork, and mix in the sour cream, milk, melted butter, and vanilla. Blend these together well, add all at once to the dry ingredients, and stir just until moistened. Do not beat.

Spoon the batter into a well greased 13 x 9 x 2-inch pan. Spread the topping evenly over the batter, and bake in a preheated 350° oven for 35 to 45 minutes or until done.

Note: This cake can also be made in a 10-inch tube pan, but baking time may have to be adjusted upward.

Blueberry Sour Cream Coffee Cake

 Makes two large cakes. This is so delicious! It was a favorite with all my patrons and is a great choice if you want something special to give or to serve.

Cream together in large mixing bowl:
    2 sticks (1 cup) butter or margarine
    1 tsp. salt
    2 cups sugar
    2 tsp. vanilla
Add one at a time:
    4 eggs
Mix together:
    4 cups all-purpose flour
    2 tsp. baking soda
    2 tsp. baking powder
Add this to creamed mixture alternately with:
    2 cups sour cream (16-oz. container)

Fold in:
    4 cups blueberries (fresh or frozen) mixed with:
    2 to 3 Tbsp. extra flour

Grease well two 9- or 10-inch tube or bundt pans, and sprinkle the bottoms with either flour or chopped nuts. Into each pan, spoon a layer of batter, and sprinkle with a layer of streusel. Divide the remaining batter and place in pans, covering the layer of streusel. Lastly, divide the remaining streusel and cover the tops of the cakes.

Streusel Topping in Layers:

Mix together:
    1 cup sugar (brown or white or both)
    2 tsp. cinnamon
    1 cup chopped walnuts or pecans

Bake the two cakes in a preheated 350° oven for 45 to 60 minutes. Be sure to test before removing from oven.

Note: Raspberries (fresh or frozen, without juice) may be used in place of the blueberries. The fruit may be added in the frozen state.

Mother Adams's Blueberry
Coffee Cake

Cake:

3/4 cup sugar
1/4 cup shortening
1 egg
2 cups all-purpose flour
2 tsp. baking powder
1/2 tsp. salt
1/2 cup milk
2 cups blueberries

Combine sugar, shortening, and egg; beat well. Sift together flour, baking powder, and salt; add to first mixture alternately with milk, mixing until well blended. Fold in the blueberries.

Spoon into a greased and floured 9- or 10-inch tube pan or well-greased 8- or 9-inch square pan. Sprinkle top with the following, mixed together with a fork until crumbly:

Topping:

1/2 cup sugar
1/3 cup flour
1/4 cup softened butter
1/2 tsp. cinnamon

Bake in a preheated 350° oven for 45 to 55 minutes.

Blueberry Butter Buckle

 This can be made in one bundt pan (or 10-inch tube pan) or two loaf pans.

1 stick butter	2 extra-large eggs
1/4 cup shortening	3 cups flour
1 1/2 cups sugar	3 tsp. baking powder
1/2 tsp. salt	1 cup milk plus 2 Tbsp.
1 1/2 tsp. vanilla extract	3 cups blueberries

Cream together well the butter, shortening, sugar, salt, and vanilla. Add eggs, one at a time; beat well. Mix the flour and baking powder and add to the creamed mixture alternately with the milk. Mix until well blended. Dredge the blueberries in about 2 Tbsp. of flour, then fold berries into batter.

Put into a well-greased bundt or tube pan (or two loaf pans). Cover with Butter Streusel Topping, below.

Topping:

- 1/4 cup butter
- 1/2 cup flour
- 1/2 cup sugar (may use brown sugar)
- 1/2 tsp. cinnamon (or more)

Beat this with a mixer on low until crumbly, or mix with a fork. Pat the streusel all over the top of the batter in the pan, and circle with pecan halves.

Bake in a preheated 350° oven for 45 to 60 minutes (or longer) or until done. Be sure to test.

Note: raspberries, marionberries (extra-large blackberries), or chopped apples may be substituted. You can use either fresh or frozen berries. If you are using apples, add a little cinnamon, nutmeg, and lemon juice to the batter.

Sour Cream Blueberry Butter Buckle

 This makes enough for two 10-inch bundt or tube pans.

1 cup chopped nuts	4 cups all-purpose flour
2 sticks butter	2 tsp. baking powder
2 cups sugar	2 tsp. baking soda
$^1/_2$ tsp. salt	2 cups sour cream (1 pint)
4 large eggs	4 cups blueberries
3 tsp. vanilla extract	

Butter the bottoms of the pans, then sprinkle with chopped nuts.

Cream together well the butter, sugar, and salt. Add eggs one at a time until well blended. Add vanilla. Mix flour, baking powder, and baking soda together; add to creamed mixture alternately with the sour cream until well blended, ending with flour mixture. Dredge blueberries in about 2 Tbsp. flour, and fold in.

Divide batter evenly between the two pans and cover the tops with butter streusel topping.

Butter Streusel Topping:

1 cup flour
1 cup sugar
1 stick butter
2 tsp. cinnamon

Beat with a mixer on low until crumbly.

Pat this all over the tops of the two cakes, and circle with pecan halves. Bake in a preheated 350° oven for 45 to 60 minutes (or longer) or until done.

Note: Raspberries or apples may be substituted for the blueberries. If you use apples, be sure to add a little nutmeg, cinnamon, and lemon juice to the batter, along with the vanilla.

Apple Butter Buckle

 This cake appeared in both the Maine Times *and the* New England Travel Guide *in the 1980s.*

Streusel for Topping:

> $^1/_2$ stick butter
> $^1/_2$ cup brown sugar or granulated sugar
> $^1/_2$ cup flour
> 1 tsp. cinnamon

Mix all together with a fork until crumbly. Set aside.

Cake:

> 1 $^1/_2$ sticks butter
> $^1/_2$ tsp. salt
> 1 cup sugar

Cream this well.

Add:

> 2 extra-large eggs, one at a time, mixing in well.

Add:

> 2 cups all-purpose flour
> 1 tsp. baking powder
> 1 tsp. baking soda
> $^1/_2$ tsp. cinnamon
> $^1/_4$ tsp. nutmeg
> $^1/_2$ tsp. lemon extract

Alternately with:

> 1 cup sour cream, beating well

Fold in:

> 3 cups peeled, chopped apples (your choice—I like Golden Delicious)

Mixed with:

> 1 Tbsp. flour
> $^1/_8$ tsp. cinnamon
> $^1/_8$ tsp. nutmeg

Turn into a greased and floured 9- or 10-inch tube or bundt pan. Cover the top with streusel, patting down with a spoon. Circle with pecan halves. Bake in a preheated 350° oven for one hour or longer. Be sure to test with cake tester or toothpick. When tester comes out absolutely clean, cake is done.

Cranberry Sour Cream Coffee Cake

 Makes two tube or bundt cakes. This treat has been very popular during the holidays.

Streusel Topping (applied in layers):

Mix together and set aside:

    1 cup brown sugar

    2 tsp. cinnamon

    1 cup chopped walnuts or pecans

Cake:

    2 sticks (1 cup) butter or margarine

    1 tsp. salt

    2 cups sugar

    2 tsp. vanilla

    4 eggs

    4 cups all-purpose flour

    2 tsp. baking soda

    2 tsp. baking powder

    2 cups sour cream (16-oz. container)

    1 (16 oz.) can whole cranberry sauce

In a large mixing bowl, cream together the butter, salt, sugar, and vanilla until light and fluffy. Add eggs, one at a time, until well blended. Mix together the flour, baking soda, and baking powder; add to the creamed mixture alternately with sour cream, ending with dry ingredients. In a separate bowl, stir the cranberry sauce to smooth the lumps.

Use two 9- or 10-inch tube or bundt pans (with solid bottoms). Grease well and sprinkle bottoms of pans with either flour or chopped nuts. Into each pan spoon a layer of batter. Divide the cranberry sauce in half and spoon over the batter in the two pans; next, sprinkle the sauce with some of the streusel (leave enough for final topping). Use the remaining batter, dividing between the two pans, to cover the sauce and streusel. Cover the tops generously with the remaining streusel.

Bake in a preheated 350° oven for about 45 to 55 minutes, being sure to check for doneness with a cake tester or toothpick before removing from oven. Let cool in pans for 15 to 20 minutes. Loosen cakes from sides and tubes with a straight table knife. Cover the cake with a piece of waxed paper (to keep the streusel intact) and put a second piece over a cake rack. Tip the cake and turn right side up with the streusel on top. Cool completely before wrapping.

Cream Cheese and Butter Crumb Cake

Crumb Topping:

$^1/_4$ cup butter or margarine
$^1/_2$ cup flour
$^1/_2$ cup brown sugar

Cake:

1 stick butter or margarine
1 (8 oz.) pkg. cream cheese
$^1/_2$ tsp. salt
1$^1/_4$ cups sugar
2 eggs
1 tsp. vanilla
2 cups flour
2 tsp. baking powder
$^1/_2$ tsp. baking soda
$^1/_2$ cup milk

Thoroughly cream together the butter, cream cheese, and salt. Add the sugar slowly, creaming well. Add eggs, one at a time, and vanilla. Sift together the flour, baking powder, and baking soda. Add to creamed mixture alternately with milk, mixing well.

If you are using a 9- or 10-inch tube pan (greased), pour the batter in two layers, with the crumb topping in the center and on top. Bake in a preheated 350° oven 40 to 50 minutes. If using a 13 x 9 x 2-inch greased pan, sprinkle the crumb topping just on the top, and bake in a preheated 350° oven 30 to 35 minutes.

Optional: drizzle top with lemon glaze, below, after removing cake from oven.

Lemon Glaze:

confectioners' sugar
lemon juice or concentrated lemonade
boiling water

Mix together to make a thin glaze.

Pineapple Swirl Coffee Cake

Cake:

1 (8³/₄ oz.) can crushed pineapple
¹/₃ cup shortening
¹/₂ cup sugar
1 egg
1 tsp. vanilla
1¹/₄ cups all-purpose flour
1¹/₂ tsp. baking powder
¹/₄ tsp. salt

Topping:

¹/₃ cup brown sugar
3 Tbsp. butter or margarine, melted
¹/₂ cup flaked coconut
¹/₃ cup chopped nuts

Drain pineapple well, reserving ¹/₂ cup syrup. Cream shortening and sugar. Add egg and vanilla; beat until light and fluffy. Sift together flour, baking powder and salt; add to creamed mixture alternately with reserved syrup, beginning and ending with flour mixture.

Spread half of batter in a greased 8 x 8 x 2-inch baking pan; spread with drained pineapple. Top with remaining batter. Combine topping ingredients; sprinkle over all. Bake in a preheated 350° oven for about 35 to 45 minutes.

Note: If you don't have ¹/₂ cup juice from the pineapple, add water or orange juice to make up the difference.

Butter Streusel Topping

 This can be used on the top of any butter-type cake or coffee cake.

1 stick butter, softened
1 cup flour
1 cup sugar, half brown, half white
2 tsp. cinnamon
zest of 1 lemon or 1 orange

This may be mixed with a pastry blender, a mixer, a fork, or even your fingers until it looks like crumbs.

Sugar-Cinnamon Nut Streusel

 This streusel is nice used in layers for a coffee cake or a butter-type cake.

1 cup sugar, brown or white
1 cup chopped pecans or walnuts or almonds
1 Tbsp. cinnamon

Mix in a bowl with a cover, and have it ready for a cake when time is of the essence.

Note: Chocolate bits or shredded coconut may be added if desired.

Yeast Breads & Rolls

Oatmeal Yeast Bread
#1

 This was a big favorite of my two sons, and it was a regular in our household.

Into a large bowl, put:
  1 cup rolled oats
  2 tsp. salt
  $^1/_2$ cup molasses
  $^1/_3$ cup oil

Add:
  2 cups boiling water or coffee
Stir all ingredients to blend thoroughly.

When lukewarm, add:
  2 eggs, well beaten
  2 pkg. dry yeast

When yeast is dissolved, add:
  $4^1/_2$ cups flour (or more)
Mix in with a spoon.

Let this stand (no kneading) for about 15 to 20 minutes. Now turn it out on a floured board, knead well, and then cut into four parts. Form into balls and put two into each of two large, well buttered bread pans and let rise until doubled. Bake in a preheated 375° oven for 35 to 45 minutes. Brush tops with butter, remove from pans, and place on a rack to cool.

Oatmeal Yeast Bread
#2

This is delicious!

2 cups dry oatmeal
4 cups boiling water (or coffee)
2 yeast cakes or 2 pkg. dry yeast
1 cup lukewarm water
1 cup molasses
2 tsp. salt
6 Tbsp. melted butter
11 to 12 cups flour

Grease a large bowl with butter or margarine. Add oatmeal, then pour in boiling water (or coffee). Let stand for 20 minutes.

In the meantime, dissolve yeast cakes or dry yeast in lukewarm water. Add to cooled oatmeal mixture at end of 20 minutes.

After the yeast, add molasses, salt, melted butter, and flour to the oatmeal mixture. Use all the flour the mixture will take; add until it takes no more. Be sure it is well blended.

Cover bowl and let the dough rise until doubled in size. Stir the dough down and let it rise again. Turn out onto a floured board. Whack down, using edge of hand, and allow the dough to relax for 10 minutes. Not much kneading; just sort of punch it around.

Shape into three or four loaves. Let rise in pans until about doubled, but not too high. Bake in preheated 350° oven for 50 minutes. If you want to use part of the dough for rolls, bake these in a 400° oven for 20 minutes.

Chris McMahon's
All-Bran Yeast Bread

1 pkg. dry yeast
2 cups warm water
$^1/4$ cup molasses
1 egg, beaten

$^1/2$ cup All-Bran cereal
$^1/4$ cup melted shortening
1 tsp. salt
6 cups flour

Dissolve yeast in warm water. Add molasses, beaten egg, and All-Bran. Mix well and add remaining ingredients. Blend thoroughly. Turn out on floured board, knead well, and let rise until double. Punch down, and let rise again. Make into two loaves or form into two dozen balls if making rolls. Let rise until double. Bake in preheated 350° oven for 30 minutes for loaves or 400° for 25 minutes for rolls.

Pumpernickel Bread

3 pkg. dry yeast
$1^1/2$ cups warm water
2 Tbsp. shortening
4 tsp. salt
$^1/2$ cup molasses
2 Tbsp. caraway seeds
$2^3/4$ cups rye flour
$2^3/4$ to $3^1/4$ cups all-purpose or bread flour
cornmeal

In a large bowl, dissolve yeast in warm water. Add the shortening, salt, molasses, and seeds. Mix well. Add the flour (both kinds) 1 cup at a time, mixing by hand until you have a nice dough. Turn it out onto a floured board, and knead until dough is smooth. Form into a ball, cover with a cloth, and let rise until double; punch down and allow dough to rise again.

Grease baking sheet; sprinkle with cornmeal. Divide dough in half. Shape each half into round, slightly flattened loaves. Place loaves in opposite corners of large cookie sheet. Butter the tops; cover; let rise 1 hour. Heat oven to 375°. Bake 30 to 35 minutes or until fully baked. Tap the bottom of the loaves; if they sound hollow, they are done.

Shredded Wheat Bread

 One of many wonderful recipes given to me by my friend Elizabeth Johnson of Portland, Maine.

2 ^{1}/$_2$ shredded wheat biscuits
1 ^{1}/$_2$ Tbsp. shortening
2 ^{1}/$_2$ cups boiling water

2 Tbsp. sugar
1 Tbsp. salt

Mix together above ingredients, let cool, then add ^{1}/$_2$ cup molasses and one yeast cake dissolved in ^{1}/$_3$ cup lukewarm water. With a spoon, mix in 6 cups of flour. Let rise in mixing bowl; cover; punch down. Put in 2 greased loaf pans and let rise. Bake in a preheated 375° oven for 45 minutes.

Jule Kake

("Christmas Cake," or Norwegian Sweet Bread)

 I was first introduced to this delicious bread by my dear friend Ginny Bicknell of Rockland, Maine. We used to receive one of these for Christmas from Ginny and her family. It was always my favorite.

Put in mixing bowl:
   2 cups flour
   1 cup sugar
   2 pkg. dry yeast
   1 ^{1}/$_2$ tsp. salt
   1 tsp. cardamom, ground
Scald in a saucepan:
   2 cups milk
   4 Tbsp. butter, margarine, or shortening
Add to dry mixture with:
   2 eggs
   1 cup raisins
   ^{1}/$_2$ cup citron
Beat 3 minutes; then add:
   5 cups flour

Let rise twice. Shape into 2 or 3 round loaves. Let rise again. Bake in preheated 350° oven for 30 to 40 minutes until brown.

Sweet Yeast Dough

 This is good for braids, rolls, and stollen. Raisins and/or other dried fruits may be added to taste. Add some cardamom (with the flour) if you're going to make Finnish nissua.

3 cups milk	1 cup butter or margarine
1 cup sugar	4 pkg. dry yeast in 1 cup warm water
3 tsp. salt	4 extra-large eggs, lightly beaten
	15 cups flour

Heat milk with sugar, salt, and butter until scalded. Allow mixture to cool until you can comfortably test it on your wrist. Meanwhile, dissolve yeast in the warm water. Add the yeast/water mixture to the cooled milk mixture. Blend in the lightly beaten eggs and mix well. Add as much flour as needed to make a soft and slightly sticky dough. Knead on a floured board until dough is smooth, adding more flour as needed. Put dough in a large buttered bowl, then turn over so the top gets buttered, too.

Cover with a dish towel and allow to rise until doubled in size. Punch down and allow to rise again until almost doubled. Transfer dough from bowl to lightly floured board. Gently knead, then cover dough with towel and allow to rest for 10 minutes. Cut the dough into three to five pieces (depending on the size of loaf you want), and form each into a ball (one ball makes one loaf).

For braid, cut one ball into three pieces and roll each piece into long strips. Braid these, starting in the middle, until you have a neat loaf. Place the braid in a 9 x 5 x 3-inch loaf pan, or if you've made a large one, onto a greased cookie sheet. Bake in a preheated 350° oven for 25 to 35 minutes or until nicely browned.

Note: My family likes nissua frosted and decorated with pecan halves and candied cherries.

Frosting or Glaze:

1 stick butter	1 tsp. almond flavoring
1 lb. confectioners' sugar	3 to 5 Tbsp. boiling water

Melt butter, remove from heat, and add confectioners' sugar and almond flavoring, plus boiling water—as much as it takes to make a drizzly glaze. Use more sugar if needed. Drizzle this over the tops of your braids after the bread has cooled.

Nissua

Put in a mixing bowl:
   2 cups flour
   $1/2$ cup sugar
   2 pkg. dry yeast
   $1\,1/2$ tsp. salt
   1 rounded tsp. cardamom seeds, crushed

Scald in a saucepan:
   2 cups milk
   1 stick butter or margarine

Add to dry mixture with:
   2 eggs
Beat for 3 minutes.

Add:
   5 cups flour (or more)

Turn out onto a floured board and knead gently. Let rise twice. Divide dough in half or into thirds. Shape each portion into strips and braid, starting from the middle. Let rise until doubled.

   Place loaves on a greased cookie sheet, and bake in a preheated 350° oven for 20 to 30 minutes. Frost (see preceding recipe), and decorate with nuts and cherries.

Note: This bread is delicious braided with two strips of dough instead of three, and placed in a greased 9 x 5 x 3-inch loaf pan.

Mrs. Hocking's Quick and Easy Rolls

 Once you try these, you'll make them again and again because they are so easy and delicious. Arnold's mom used to whip them up all the time.

1 cup milk
1 yeast cake
2 Tbsp. sugar
1 tsp. salt
1 egg, well beaten
2 Tbsp. shortening, melted
2 1/4 cups flour

Scald milk and cool to lukewarm. Add yeast and dissolve. Add sugar, salt, beaten egg, and melted shortening. Mix well and stir in flour. Let rise to double its size. Punch down, then drop by spoonfuls into greased muffin tins (about half full). Let rise about 30 minutes and bake in a preheated 400° oven for 12 to 15 minutes. Makes 12 rolls.

Refrigerator Yeast Rolls

 When our luncheon group gets together, Chris McMahon is usually delegated to make her special rolls.

1 cup warm water (105° to 115°)
1 Tbsp. sugar
2 pkg. dry yeast
2 cups milk
2/3 cup shortening (scant)
1/2 cup sugar
4 tsp. salt
2 eggs, beaten
10 to 11 cups flour

Mix water and 1 Tbsp. sugar together, add yeast and let dissolve.
   Scald the milk and shortening; stir in the sugar and salt. Cool this mixture. Add the beaten eggs, then add the yeast mixture. Add flour, beating by hand. Knead the dough a little. Put in refrigerator in a tightly covered bowl (dough will keep this way for four or five days). Remove dough from refrigerator and form into rolls. Let rise for three hours in a warm place. Bake in a preheated 400° oven for 15 to 25 minutes.

Ruth Goldsmith's Yeast Rolls

 This recipe was given to my sister-in-law, Priscilla Adams-Smith, by Mrs. Goldsmith, her Rockland, Maine, neighbor. Note that you must make the dough a day ahead and refrigerate it overnight. The rolls are delicious!

1 cup milk
$^1/_4$ lb. butter (1 stick)
1 yeast cake in 2 Tbsp. warm water
3 egg yolks, well beaten
$^1/_8$ tsp. salt
$3^1/_2$ cups flour

Scald the milk; add the butter and allow to melt. Cool slightly. Dissolve the yeast in the warm water, then add to the milk. Mix well. Add the egg yolks, salt, and flour. Blend thoroughly, cover bowl, and refrigerate overnight.

In the morning, cut dough into four sections and roll each into a circle. Cut each circle into eight pie-shaped pieces. Roll up each piece, starting with the pointed end. Shape into a crescent. Let rise 1 hour. Bake 10 to 12 minutes in a preheated 360° oven. Makes about three dozen.

Sweet Rolls

Put in large mixing bowl:
  3 cups flour
  1 cup sugar
  2 pkg. dry yeast
  2 tsp. salt
  $^1/_2$ tsp. cinnamon (heaping)
  $^1/_2$ tsp. lemon peel
Scald in a saucepan:
  1 $^1/_4$ cups milk
  $^3/_4$ cup water
  1 stick butter, margarine, or shortening ($^1/_2$ cup)
Add to dry mixture with:
  2 eggs, unbeaten
  1 $^1/_2$ cups raisins (heaping)
Beat for three minutes; then add:
  4 to 5 cups flour (or more)

Knead well and let rise two times. Shape into rolls; let these rise until doubled. Bake in preheated 350° oven 20 to 30 minutes or until brown. Frost with a basic confectioners' sugar icing.

Quick Breads

Banana Bread

 Always moist and delicious! This recipe will make two large loaves.

Cream together well:
   1 cup shortening or 2 sticks butter
   1 tsp. salt
   2 cups sugar (you can use half white and half brown)
   1 tsp. vanilla
   $1/2$ tsp. nutmeg (optional)
Add:
   4 extra-large eggs, one at a time
Beat until well blended.

Mix together or sift:
   4 cups all-purpose flour
   2 tsp. baking soda
Add alternately with:
   1 cup mashed ripe bananas mixed with:
   1 cup buttermilk

Beat all together until well blended. Chopped nuts (2 cups) may be added if you choose. Pour into two well greased 9 x 5 x 3-inch loaf pans, and bake in a preheated 325° oven for about one hour.

Banana Date Nut Bread

 Another goody from my friend and former college roommate Elizabeth (Liz) Johnson.

In large bowl mix:
    1 3/4 cups all-purpose flour
    1 1/2 cups sugar
    1 tsp. double-acting baking powder
    1/2 tsp. salt
    1/4 tsp. baking soda
Cut in:
    1/2 cup butter or margarine
Stir in:
    1 cup mashed bananas (two very ripe, medium size)
    1 cup pitted dates, chopped
    1 cup chopped nuts
    2 eggs, slightly beaten

Bake in greased 8 x 4 1/2 x 2 1/2-inch pan for 1 hour and 15 minutes in 350° preheated oven. Cool in pan on wire rack for 10 minutes. Remove and finish cooling on rack.

My Mother's Date Nut Bread

 Delicious for sandwiches when spread with cream cheese. My mother made this frequently.

3/4 cup chopped walnuts
1 cup cut dates
1 1/2 tsp. baking soda
1/2 tsp. salt
3 Tbsp. shortening or butter, melted
3/4 cup boiling water
2 eggs
1 tsp. vanilla
1 cup sugar
1 1/2 cups flour

Mix first four ingredients with fork. Add shortening and boiling water. Let stand 20 minutes. Preheat oven to 350°. Beat eggs with fork; add vanilla, sugar, and flour, beating with fork. Add date mixture. Mix just until blended. Bake in a greased 9 x 5 x 3-inch pan about 45 to 55 minutes.

Note: During the years when I was growing up, afternoon teas were very popular, especially in our home. My mother always had different sweet breads on hand, spread with cream cheese and made into small finger sandwiches. I especially remember those made with date nut bread.

Mrs. Withington's Date Bread

 This is delicious when spread with cream cheese to make sandwiches.

Combine:
 1 1/2 cups pitted, chopped dates
 1 1/2 cups boiling water
 1 tsp. of butter
Let stand.

Mix:
 1 cup sugar
 2 3/4 cups flour
 1/2 tsp. salt
 2 tsp. baking soda
 1/2 cup chopped nuts (optional)

Add dates and water to this mixture. Stir, then add:
 1 tsp. vanilla
 1 well beaten egg.

Pour batter into a well greased 9 x 5 x 3-inch loaf pan. Bake about 1 hour in a preheated 350° oven.

Note: This bread is particularly good if you add 2 tsp. instant coffee to the boiling water before combining it with the dates.

Orange-Marmalade Date Nut Bread

1 cup dates, chopped
1 cup hot water
1 Tbsp. butter
1 beaten egg
$^2/_3$ cup brown sugar

$^1/_2$ cup nuts, chopped
2 cups flour
1 tsp. soda
$^1/_4$ tsp. salt
$^1/_2$ cup orange marmalade

Combine dates, hot water, and butter; cool slightly. Add egg, sugar, and nuts. Sift flour, baking soda, and salt; add to date mixture. Stir in marmalade. Pour batter into a well greased loaf pan, and bake for about 1 hour in a preheated 350° oven.

Apricot Nut Bread

1 cup dried apricots
$2^1/_2$ cups flour
$1^1/_4$ cups sugar
2 tsp. baking powder
$^1/_2$ tsp. baking soda
$^1/_2$ tsp. salt

2 eggs, beaten
$^1/_4$ cup butter, melted
$^1/_2$ cup orange juice
2 Tbsp. grated peel
2 Tbsp. water
1 cup chopped walnuts

Cut up the apricots and put into a bowl with enough hot water to cover. Soak for about 30 minutes.

Mix flour, sugar, baking powder, baking soda, and salt. Combine eggs, melted butter, orange juice, peel, and water. Add all at once to flour mixture. Add drained apricots and mix until dry ingredients are moistened. Stir in the walnuts. Turn into greased 9 x 5 x 3-inch loaf pan.

Bake in preheated 350° oven for 1 hour or until done (check bread after 45 minutes).

Orange Nut Bread

2 1/2 cups flour
1/2 tsp. baking powder
1/4 tsp. salt
1/4 tsp. baking soda
1 cup sugar
2 eggs

1/2 cup milk
3/4 cup oil
1/2 cup orange juice
grated peel of 1 orange
1/2 cup nuts, chopped

Combine all dry ingredients. Beat eggs well; add the milk, oil, juice, and peel. Combine with dry ingredients and nuts. Pour into a greased 9 x 5 x 3-inch loaf pan. Bake in a preheated 350° oven for about 1 hour.

Note: If desired, you can mix 1/2 cup orange juice with about 1/2 cup sugar while the bread is baking. As soon as the bread is done, pour this topping all over the bread while it is still in pan. When liquid is absorbed, remove bread from pan. A little sprinkling of additional sugar may be used to make a crunchy topping.

Strawberry Pecan Bread

A nice way to use those yummy fresh strawberries!

Mix dry ingredients in a large bowl:
   3 cups flour
   3/4 tsp. salt
   1 1/2 cups sugar
   1 tsp. baking soda
   2 tsp. cinnamon
   1 1/2 cups chopped pecans or walnuts
Blend:
   4 eggs, well-beaten
   1 1/4 cups oil
Add to dry ingredients. Mix until moistened.

Stir in:
   2 cups strawberries, mashed

Bake in two greased and floured 9 x 5 x 3-inch loaf pans in a preheated 350° oven for about 1 hour. This bread also makes nice cream cheese sandwiches.

Fresh Strawberry Bread

 This was given to me by my mother. It's so nice when you have fresh strawberries. Just mix the ingredients as you would for muffins—easy!

2 cups flour
3 tsp. baking powder
$^1/_2$ tsp. baking soda
$^1/_2$ tsp. salt
$^1/_4$ tsp. cinnamon
$^1/_4$ tsp. allspice

$^3/_4$ cup sugar
1 egg
$^1/_2$ cup milk
$^1/_3$ cup shortening, melted
$^2/_3$ cup mashed strawberries
$^1/_2$ cup chopped walnuts

Sift together all the dry ingredients. Mix the egg, milk, and shortening, and stir into dry ingredients, just enough to moisten. Add the remaining ingredients, stirring just until mixed. Pour into a greased loaf pan. Bake in a preheated 350° oven for 45 to 55 minutes.

Lemon Bread

Batter:

$^3/_4$ cup shortening
2 cups sugar
grated rind of two lemons
4 eggs, beaten
3 cups flour
1 tsp. salt
2 tsp. baking powder
1 cup milk

Glaze:

juice of 2 lemons
1 cup sugar

Cream shortening and sugar until blended. Add lemon rind and well-beaten eggs. Blend. Sift and measure flour. Resift flour with salt and baking powder; add to creamed mixture alternately with milk. Mix together. Pour batter into two greased 9 x 5 x 3-inch loaf pans. Bake in a preheated 350° oven for 40 minutes or until loaves test done. Pour glaze over bread as soon as loaves are taken from oven. Cool for 10 minutes before removing bread from pans.

Quick and Easy Lemon Bread

Combine all ingredients in large mixing bowl:

   2 Tbsp. lemonade concentrate
   1 cup shortening
   2 cups sugar
   4 large eggs
   1 cup milk
   4 tsp. baking powder
   3 cups all-purpose flour

Beat on medium speed for 3 minutes.

Pour into two well buttered 9 x 5 x 3-inch loaf pans. Bake in 350° oven 45 to 55 minutes or until done.

Glaze:

   1 (8 oz. or larger) can lemonade concentrate, thawed
   1 to 2 cups sugar

Stir these together to make a medium syrup while bread is baking. When loaves come out of the oven, poke them all over with a meat fork and loosen from sides of pan. Using a long-handled ladle, pour half of glaze over each loaf. After glaze has soaked in, sprinkle tops lightly with granulated sugar and turn loaves out of pans. Sprinkle them again with more sugar to give them crunchy tops.

Lemon Prune Nut Bread

$2^1/2$ cups flour
3 tsp. baking powder
$^1/2$ tsp. salt
1 egg, beaten
1 tsp. vanilla
$^3/4$ cup sugar

$^1/4$ cup melted butter or margarine, or oil
$1^1/4$ cups unsweetened prune juice
$^1/2$ cup dried prunes, chopped
$^1/2$ cup nuts, chopped
1 Tbsp. grated lemon peel

Preheat oven to 350°. Grease a 9 x 5 x 3-inch loaf pan. Boil prune juice and pour over prunes; let cool. Sift flour with baking powder and salt; set aside. In a large bowl, combine egg, vanilla, sugar, and butter. Using a wooden spoon or portable electric mixer, beat until well blended. Add to egg mixture, blending well. Add flour mixture, beating until smooth. Stir in nuts and lemon peel. Bake about 60 to 65 minutes. Cool in pan for 10 minutes before removing.

Lemon Nut Bread

1/2 cup shortening
1 cup sugar
2 eggs
1 1/4 cups flour
1 tsp. baking powder

1/2 tsp. salt
1/2 cup milk
3/4 cup chopped walnuts
grated rind of one lemon

Cream the shortening and 1 cup sugar, then add the eggs; beat well. Mix and sift flour, baking powder, and salt; add to the creamed mixture alternately with milk. Stir in nut meats and lemon rind. Bake in a greased 9 x 5 x 3-inch tin in a preheated 350° oven for about one hour.

Glaze:

1/4 cup sugar
juice of one lemon

Combine the 1/4 cup sugar and the lemon juice. Pour over the top of bread as soon as it is taken from the oven. Cool for at least ten minutes before removing bread from pan.

Cherry Sweet Bread

 This makes a great holiday gift, presented in a pretty tin.

2 1/2 cups flour
2 tsp. baking powder
1/2 tsp. baking soda
1 1/2 cups candied cherries, chopped
1 cup walnuts, chopped
3/4 cup butter or margarine
1 1/4 cups sugar
2 extra-large eggs
1 cup orange juice

Combine flour, baking powder, and baking soda; set aside 1 cup of mixture for dredging fruit and nuts. Combine cherries and walnuts in a large bowl. Add 1 cup reserved flour mixture and stir to coat fruit and nuts. Cream butter; add sugar gradually, beating until light and fluffy. Add eggs, one at a time, beating at medium speed after each addition. Add dry ingredients alternately with orange juice, beginning and ending with flour mixture. Fold in fruit mixture. Pour batter into a greased and floured 10-inch bundt pan.

Bake in a preheated 350° oven for 1 hour or until done. Cool bread in pan 10 minutes; remove from pan and cool completely on wire rack. Top with sifted confectioners' sugar or glaze.

Note: This can be frosted with a glaze of confectioners' sugar and orange juice and can be decorated with cherries and pecan halves.

For a different taste, you can use well-drained maraschino cherries instead of the candied cherries.

Pineapple Nut Bread

 Makes three loaves.

3 cups unsifted flour
1 tsp. baking soda
1 tsp. salt
3 tsp. nutmeg
2 cups sugar
4 eggs
1$\frac{1}{4}$ cups oil
1 (20 oz.) can crushed pineapple, with juice
1$\frac{1}{4}$ cups chopped nuts

Mix all dry ingredients and set aside. In a large bowl, beat eggs and oil; add pineapple and juice. Add nuts and all dry ingredients. Pour into three 8$\frac{1}{2}$ x 4 x 3-inch greased and floured loaf pans. Bake in a preheated 350° oven for 45 to 60 minutes. Be sure to test for doneness. Cool in pans 10 minutes before turning out.

Cranberry Nut Bread

1/2 cup shortening or butter
2 cups firmly packed light-brown sugar
2 beaten eggs
4 cups flour
1 tsp. salt
1 tsp. baking soda
3 tsp. baking powder
4 Tbsp. hot water
1 cup orange juice
2 to 3 cups halved fresh cranberries
1/2 cup chopped nuts

Cream shortening and add sugar. Beat until light; add eggs and beat well. Sift flour, salt, baking soda, and baking powder. Add alternately with combination of hot water and orange juice. Stir-in halved cranberries and nuts.

Put into two greased 9 x 5 x 3-inch loaf pans and bake for about 1 hour in a preheated 350° oven.

Quick and Easy Cranberry Nut Bread

 My mother also used this bread when making cream cheese sandwiches, and everyone just loved it. It's great for a gathering and is very easy to make.

Mix all ingredients together and stir only to moisten:
4 cups flour
2 tsp. baking soda
1 tsp. salt
1 1/2 cups sugar
2 eggs, slightly beaten
1 1/3 cups milk
1/2 cup melted butter, margarine, or oil
1 can whole cranberry sauce (2 cups)
2 cups chopped walnuts

Bake in two well greased 9 x 5 x 3-inch loaf pans in a preheated 350° oven for about 45 to 55 minutes or until done.

Blueberry Bread

 This will make two large loaves and is delicious toasted, warm from the oven and spread with butter or cream cheese, or just the way it is.

4 large eggs
1 ^{1}/3 cups sugar
^{1}/2 tsp. salt
^{1}/4 tsp. cinnamon
^{1}/2 cup oil
1 ^{1}/3 cups milk
1 tsp. vanilla
^{1}/2 tsp. lemon extract
4 slightly heaping cups flour
4 tsp. baking powder
4 cups fresh blueberries
pecan halves for tops
sugar to sprinkle

Beat eggs until light in color; add sugar, salt, and cinnamon. Beat this well. Add oil, milk, vanilla, and lemon extract. Beat these until well blended. Last, add flour and baking powder, beating just until mixed. Toss blueberries with a little extra flour and fold into bread mixture.

Pour into two well greased 9 x 5 x 3-inch loaf pans. Cover tops with pecan halves, and sprinkle with sugar. Bake in a preheated 350° oven for about 1 hour or until done. The recipe may be halved successfully.

Berry Loaf

 Use either blueberries, raspberries, marionberries (extra-large blackberries), or all three.

2 sticks butter, softened
1 1/2 cups sugar
3 large eggs
4 tsp. baking powder
1 tsp. salt
1/4 tsp. cinnamon
4 cups all-purpose flour
1 cup plus 2 Tbsp. milk
2 tsp. vanilla
3 cups berries, fresh or frozen (unthawed)
pecan halves for tops
sugar to sprinkle

In large mixing bowl, thoroughly cream the butter and sugar, then add the eggs one at a time. In another bowl, stir or sift together all the dry ingredients; add alternately to the egg mixture with the combined milk and vanilla. Fold berries in last (if you like lots of berries, just increase the amount). Pour into two well greased 9 x 5 x 3-inch loaf pans. Sprinkle the tops of the loaves with pecan halves and granulated sugar.

Bake in preheated 350° oven for about 45 minutes or until done. This bread tastes best if it's warmed up in either the oven or microwave.

Prune Bread

1/2 lb. dried prunes
3/4 cup boiling water
1 3/4 cups flour
3/4 cup sugar
1 tsp. baking soda
1/2 tsp. salt
1 egg, beaten
2 Tbsp. melted shortening or oil
1 tsp. vanilla

Soak prunes in cold water for 2 hours; drain, pit, and chop prunes. Add boiling water and let stand for 5 minutes. Sift together flour, sugar, baking soda, and salt. Add prune mixture. Add beaten egg, then add shortening (or oil) and vanilla. Mix well. Pour into a greased loaf pan, 8^1/$_2$ x 4^1/$_2$ x 2^1/$_2$ inches. Bake at 325° in preheated oven for about 1 hour. Remove from pan and cool on wire rack.

Note: This recipe may be doubled with success.

Pumpkin Bread

 There are many excellent variations for pumpkin bread, so I am putting a few down for you to try. They have all been favorites with my patrons, especially during the holidays.

Cream together:
   1 cup oil
   3 cups sugar

Add, one at a time:
   4 eggs

Mix in:
   2 cups mashed cooked pumpkin (or a 16-oz. can prepared pumpkin)

Sift together or mix:
   3^1/$_2$ cups flour
   2 tsp. baking soda
   1 tsp. baking powder
   2 tsp. salt
   1 tsp. nutmeg
   1 tsp. cinnamon
   1 tsp. allspice
   ^{1}/$_4$ tsp. cloves
   ^{1}/$_4$ tsp. ginger

Add this to the creamed mixture alternately with:
   ^{2}/$_3$ cup cold water

Bake in two greased 9 x 5 x 3-inch loaf pans in a preheated 350° oven for about 45 to 55 minutes or until the bread tests done. Two cups chopped nuts may be added if desired.

Pumpkin Bread with Chocolate Chips

 Arnold and I really like this loaf. I hope you will try it and enjoy it as much as we do.

1 stick butter ($^1/_2$ cup)
$^1/_2$ cup shortening
1 tsp. salt
$2^1/_2$ cups sugar
4 extra-large eggs
1 tsp. cinnamon
$^1/_2$ tsp. nutmeg
$^1/_4$ tsp. cloves
$^1/_4$ tsp. ginger
4 cups all-purpose flour
2 tsp. baking soda
1 tsp. baking powder
2 cups mashed cooked pumpkin, mixed with $^1/_2$ cup water
2 tsp. vanilla
2 cups mini chocolate chips
pecan halves for tops
sugar for sprinkling

Thoroughly cream together the butter, shortening, salt, and sugar. Add the eggs, one at a time, beating until well blended. Mix together the spices, flour, baking soda, and baking powder; add alternately to the creamed mixture with the pumpkin mixture and vanilla. Mix well. Fold in the chocolate chips.

Divide between two well-greased 9 x 5 x 3-inch pans. Cover the tops with pecan halves, and sprinkle all over with sugar. Bake in a 350° pre-heated oven for 50 to 60 minutes, longer if needed. Be sure to test with a cake tester or toothpick. Enjoy this bread just plain, or you can spread it with cream cheese. It freezes very well.

Pumpkin Nut Bread

2 cups flour
2 tsp. baking powder
$1/2$ tsp. baking soda
1 tsp. cinnamon
$1/2$ tsp. nutmeg
$1/4$ tsp. ginger
$1/2$ tsp. salt

1 cup cooked, mashed pumpkin
1 cup sugar
$1/2$ cup milk
2 eggs
$1/4$ cup butter or margarine, softened
$1/2$ cup chopped nuts

Sift all dry ingredients, except sugar. In a large bowl, combine pumpkin, sugar, milk, eggs, and butter. Beat until well blended.

Add flour mixture, mixing until just smooth. Stir in nuts. Pour batter into well greased and floured 9 x 5 x 3-inch loaf pan. Bake 50 to 60 minutes in a preheated 350° oven. Cool and sprinkle with confectioners' sugar, if desired.

Note: This recipe can be doubled with success.

Quick Monkey Bread

$1/2$ cup chopped pecans or halves
$1/2$ cup sugar
1 tsp. cinnamon
3 (10 oz.) cans refrigerator buttermilk biscuits
$1/2$ cup butter or margarine
1 cup packed brown sugar

Sprinkle pecans evenly in bottom of a well greased 10-inch tube, or bundt, pan. Set pan aside. Combine sugar and cinnamon. Cut biscuits into quarters; roll each piece in sugar mixture and layer in pan. Melt the butter and brown sugar in a saucepan; pour over dough.

Bake in a preheated 350° oven for 30 to 40 minutes. Cool bread for 10 minutes in the pan; invert onto serving platter. To serve, break the balls apart with two forks.

Note: Additional pecan halves and/or raisins may be sprinkled in the pan as you layer the pieces of biscuit dough.

Poppy-Seed Bread
#1

This makes a good afternoon tea cake.

3 cups flour
$1^{1}/_{2}$ tsp. baking powder
$^{1}/_{2}$ tsp. salt
$2^{1}/_{2}$ cups sugar
$1^{1}/_{2}$ cups milk

$1^{1}/_{3}$ cups oil
3 eggs
$1^{1}/_{2}$ Tbsp. poppy seeds
$1^{1}/_{2}$ tsp. vanilla
$1^{1}/_{2}$ tsp. almond extract

Mix all ingredients together; beat for 2 minutes. Bake in two greased and floured bread pans. Bake in a preheated 350° oven for 50 to 60 minutes, or until bread tests done. Allow to cool, then glaze.

Glaze:

$^{3}/_{4}$ cup confectioners' sugar
2 Tbsp. butter
$^{1}/_{2}$ tsp. almond extract
milk or water

Poppy-Seed Bread
#2

4 eggs
2 cups sugar
$1^{1}/_{2}$ tsp. vanilla
1 (14 oz.) can evaporated milk
$1^{1}/_{2}$ cups oil

3 cups flour
4 tsp. baking powder
1 tsp. salt
$^{1}/_{2}$ cup poppy seeds

Beat eggs until light and thick; add sugar and vanilla and continue beating. Gradually add evaporated milk and oil, beating well. Add flour, baking powder, and salt, beating continuously. Stir in poppy seeds. Pour into three greased 8 x 4 x 3-inch loaf pans and bake for 50 to 60 minutes in preheated 350° oven.

No-Yeast Stollen

2$\frac{1}{2}$ cups flour
$\frac{3}{4}$ cup sugar
3 tsp. baking powder
$\frac{1}{2}$ tsp. ground cardamom
$\frac{1}{2}$ tsp. salt
1 stick butter, well chilled
1 cup cottage cheese
1 egg
1 tsp. vanilla
$\frac{1}{2}$ cup raisins
3 Tbsp. butter, melted
confectioners' sugar

Grease a baking sheet. Sift the first five ingredients into large bowl. Cut the butter into the sifted flour mixture with a pastry blender or two knives until coarse crumbs form.

Mix together the cottage cheese, egg, and vanilla in a medium-size bowl. Add to the flour mixture along with the raisins. Stir until dough forms. Turn out onto a lightly floured board. Knead about ten turns, adding more flour if necessary to prevent sticking. The dough should be soft, not stiff. Roll the dough into a 10-inch circle. Brush with one table-spoon of the melted butter. Fold the dough in half just off center. Place on the greased baking sheet.

Bake 40 to 50 minutes or until golden brown in preheated 350° oven. Brush with the remaining 2 tablespoons of melted butter while hot. Cool on a wire rack.

Wrap in aluminum foil or plastic wrap when completely cooled. Store at room temperature two days before serving. Sprinkle with confectioners' sugar just before serving, if you wish. The stollen will keep for up to one week.

Spoon Bread

 Makes 4 to 6 helpings. Serve hot in place of potatoes or rolls.

5 eggs
4 tsp. baking powder
1/4 cup white cornmeal
1 Tbsp. sugar

1/2 tsp. salt
2 cups milk
2 Tbsp. melted butter or margarine

Grease a 6-cup baking dish. In a medium-size bowl, beat the eggs with the baking powder until foamy. Stir in the cornmeal, sugar, salt, milk, and melted butter. Pour into the prepared dish. Bake in preheated 350° oven for 40 minutes or until puffed and golden.

Pies & Pastry

Basic Pie Crust

 This recipe makes 2 crusts.

2³/₄ cups flour
1 tsp. salt
1 cup shortening (or part butter, part shortening)
4 to 6 Tbsp. cold water

With a pastry blender, cut the flour with the salt and shortening until the mixture is the size of peas. Add the cold water, mixing with a fork, one tablespoon at a time. Add water until pastry just stays together when pressed into a ball.

Cover dough with plastic wrap, and put it in the refrigerator for about 30 to 60 minutes. When you're ready to use it, place pastry on a lightly floured board and knead gently. Cut it in half, and roll out for the bottom crust. Save the other half to roll out for the top crust.

Butter Pie Crust

 This is a good crust to make if you're in a hurry and have a blender or food processor to mix all the ingredients. Makes one 9-inch pie crust.

1 stick (cold) butter
1 cup flour
$^1/_4$ tsp. salt
2 to 3 Tbsp. ice water
1 tsp. lemon juice

To mix in a food processor or blender, cut butter into small chunks and place in machine with flour and salt. Pulse until mixture becomes crumbly. Slowly add ice water and lemon juice until dough forms a ball. Pat into pie plate, bringing it up on the sides, or refrigerate until you are ready to roll it out.

Foolproof Pie Crust

4 cups flour, lightly spooned into measuring cup
1 Tbsp. sugar
2 tsp. salt
$1^3/_4$ cups shortening
$^1/_2$ cup water
1 Tbsp. white or cider vinegar
1 large egg

In a large bowl, stir together flour, sugar, and salt with a fork. Using the same fork, cut in shortening until crumbly. In a small bowl, beat together water, vinegar, and egg; add to flour mixture and stir until all ingredients are moistened. Divide dough into five portions, and shape each by hand into a flat, round patty ready for rolling. Wrap each patty in plastic or wax paper, and chill for at least $^1/_2$ hour.

Recipe makes two double crusts plus one single crust.

Elvie Berry's Pastry

 Priscilla Adams-Smith, my sister by marriage, says pies made with this crust have always gotten raves.

2$^1/_2$ cups flour
1 tsp. salt
1 cup lard (or Crisco shortening)
$^1/_2$ cup milk and 1 Tbsp. vinegar
1 beaten egg yolk or whole egg, for glaze

Add salt to flour. With two knives or pastry blender, cut lard into flour until coarse. Add milk mixture all at once. Stir with a fork.

Put half of mix aside for bottom crust. Pat down remaining dough, spread top with 1 additional Tbsp. lard or shortening, and fold over on itself. Press down, then spread with a bit more lard and fold again. Let this dough rest 5 minutes while rolling out bottom crust.

Roll out bottom crust. Place in pie plate, add selected filling. Roll out top crust and affix to pie. Brush top with beaten egg. Bake in a preheated 425° to 450° oven until crust is sealed (about 8 to 12 minutes). Lower heat to 350° for remaining time, baking a total of 1 hour.

Custard Pie

1 single, unbaked 9-inch deep-dish pie crust
4 eggs, slightly beaten
$^1/_2$ cup sugar
$^1/_8$ tsp. salt
3 cups milk
1 tsp. vanilla
nutmeg for garnish

Combine all ingredients except nutmeg, and mix with a whisk. Pour into pie shell and shake nutmeg over top. Bake in a preheated 450° oven for 10 minutes, then lower oven temperature to 350° and bake for 30 more minutes or until done.

Note: I also make this as a baked custard, without the crust. I leave out the nutmeg, add caramel flavoring (1$^1/_2$ tsp.), and put it into a casserole instead of a crust. Place casserole in a shallow pan of hot water, and bake in a preheated 350° oven for about 45 to 50 minutes. I always use less sugar: $^1/_4$ to $^1/_3$ cup.

Marilyn Bergman's Key Lime Pie

Crust:

18 small graham crackers
$1/4$ lb. butter, melted
$1/8$ tsp. cinnamon
$1/3$ cup sugar

Crumble crackers; add melted butter, cinnamon, and sugar. Pat into a 9-inch pie plate. Bake 20 minutes.

Filling:

1 can condensed milk
3 eggs, separated
$1/3$ cup fresh Key lime juice (or substitute regular limes)
grated rind of the limes
1 drop dark green food coloring
1 cup heavy cream, whipped

Mix condensed milk with the beaten egg yolks, lime juice, and rind (reserve a little). Add a drop of green food coloring. Beat whites and fold in. Bake for 10 minutes in preheated 250° oven. Cool and refrigerate. Top with whipped cream and sprinkle with reserved rind.

Marsha Hennessey's Key Lime Pie

vanilla wafers
1 can condensed milk
$1/2$ cup freshly squeezed Key lime juice (or substitute regular limes)
3 large eggs, separated
2 to 3 drops green food coloring
$1/4$ cup (approximately) sugar

Grease 9-inch pie plate with butter or margarine. Crush enough vanilla wafers to make a nice, thick bottom crust and line sides of pie plate with additional whole vanilla wafers. In a bowl, mix condensed milk, lime juice, egg yolks, and food coloring, stirring until well mixed. Set aside.

Beat egg whites until stiff peaks form. Add sugar, a little at a time, until well mixed. Pour lime mixture into pie plate, top with egg whites, and bake in a preheated 375° oven for 5 to 7 minutes or until golden brown. Cool on wire rack and refrigerate before serving.

Eleanor Mathieson's Party Pie

 Eleanor is an excellent cook!

Meringue Crust:

4 egg whites
$1/2$ tsp. cream of tartar
$1/8$ tsp. salt
1 cup sugar
$1/2$ tsp. vanilla

Beat egg whites and cream of tartar until foamy; beat in salt and sugar, 1 tablespoon at a time. Continue beating until stiff and glossy; do not underbeat. Beat in vanilla. When very stiff, spread in a buttered 9-inch pie plate, pressing meringue up against sides. Bake in a preheated 275° oven until dry and firm to the touch, 1 full hour.

Filling:

In double boiler, combine:

4 egg yolks
$1/2$ cup sugar
2 Tbsp. lemon juice
$1/8$ tsp. salt
$1/4$ cup crushed pineapple, pulp and syrup
grated rind from 1 lemon

Stir constantly over boiling water until thick and smooth. Cool and then spread over meringue, keeping it toward center.

Topping:

In a small bowl, whip

$3/4$ cup cream

With:

2 Tbsp. sugar and
$1/2$ tsp. vanilla
$1/4$ cup coconut (optional)

Fold in coconut, if desired. Spread over top of filling. Sprinkle with another $1/4$ cup coconut, if desired. Place in refrigerator, and chill.

Sliced-Pumpkin Pie

 This recipe was sent to me by my sister-in-law Erdine (Deanie) Hocking Ramsdell, from York, Maine.

dough for double 9-inch pie crust
4 cups pumpkin slices (peel and cut thin, similar to apple slices)
1 cup sugar
$^1/_8$ tsp. salt
1 tsp. lemon extract or 1 Tbsp. lemon juice
butter

Prepare pie crust. In bottom shell, place sliced pumpkin; sprinkle with sugar, salt, and 8 to 10 drops of lemon extract or 1 Tbsp. real lemon juice over the top. Dot with butter, and cover with top crust. Bake in a preheated 425° oven for 15 minutes, then reduce heat to 350° and finish baking for about 45 minutes.

Angel Pie

About forty or fifty years ago, this was a very popular dessert and party treat. It's still well worth making for a special dessert.

Beat together until frothy:
  3 egg whites
  $^3/_4$ tsp. lemon juice or $^1/_4$ tsp. cream of tartar
Gradually beat in, a little at a time:
  1 cup sugar

Beat until very stiff and glossy. Turn into unbuttered 9-inch pie plate and spread from middle up sides. Bake until delicately browned and crusty in a 275° oven (about 60 minutes). Turn off oven and leave crust in until oven has cooled (this finishes the baking).

Whip until stiff:
  1 cup whipping cream
Spread half over meringue shell. Cover with cooled Lemon Custard Filling (page 56). Top with remaining whipped cream. Chill about 12 hours before serving.

Walnut Pie

1 single, unbaked 9-inch deep-dish shell
1/2 cup firmly packed brown sugar
2 Tbsp. flour
1 1/4 cups light corn syrup
3 Tbsp. butter
1/4 tsp. salt
3 eggs
1 1/2 tsp. vanilla
1 cup large pieces of walnuts (or pecans)

Mix brown sugar and flour in a saucepan. Add corn syrup, butter, and salt; cook on low heat just until butter is melted. Beat eggs with vanilla, and stir into sugar mixture. Turn into pie shell, and sprinkle with walnut pieces. Bake in a preheated 375° oven for 40 to 45 minutes or until filling is set in the center.

Pecan Pie

1 single, unbaked 9-inch deep-dish pie shell
1 stick butter (no substitute)
1/8 tsp. salt
1 cup sugar
1 cup corn syrup
1 1/2 tsp. vanilla
4 large eggs
1 1/2 cups pecan halves (or chopped)

Melt butter with salt. Add sugar and corn syrup, mixing well. Add vanilla. Add eggs, beating in one at a time. Stir in pecans. Pour mixture into pie shell. Bake in preheated 375° oven for 40 minutes. (You may want to lower the oven temperature to 350° after 30 minutes.) The pie will be baked when the filling puffs up (it will later deflate).

Note: This pie is delicious served with whipped cream or ice cream.

Chocolate Pecan Pie

 Ladies Home Journal *used this recipe in the October 1996 issue. The pie was a huge favorite in my shop and among my mail-order customers.*

Melt in saucepan:
    1 stick butter
    3 squares baking chocolate, unsweetened
    $^1/_8$ tsp. salt
Remove from burner and allow to cool for about 15 minutes.

Add:
    1 cup sugar
    1 cup dark corn syrup
    2 tsp. pure vanilla (or 1 tsp. vanilla and 1 tsp. bourbon)
Mix this well with a spoon.

Add:
    3 extra-large eggs or 4 large eggs
Mix in well with a spoon after each addition.

Mix in:
    1 $^1/_2$ cups pecan halves

Pour the batter into a 9-inch deep-dish pie shell, and bake in a preheated 375° oven. After the pie has baked for 30 minutes, lower the oven temperature to 350° so as not to get the crust too brown. Let pie bake for about 10 more minutes, until the center puffs up (it will deflate as the pie cools).
    Serve with whipped cream or ice cream.

Chocolate Pecan Chess Pie

1 single, unbaked 9-inch deep-dish shell
3 eggs
1 cup sugar
$^1/_2$ cup firmly packed brown sugar
$^1/_2$ cup chocolate syrup
$^1/_4$ cup melted butter
2 Tbsp. cornstarch
1 cup pecan halves
$^1/_2$ cup heavy cream, whipped

Beat eggs slightly; stir in sugars, chocolate syrup, butter, and cornstarch. Pour into prepared shell, and arrange pecan halves on top. Bake in a preheated 425° oven for 10 minutes. Lower oven temperature to 325°, and continue baking for 35 minutes or until the center is almost set but still soft; do not overbake. Decorate with whipped cream.

Sugar Plum Mince Pie

2 cups (about 12 oz.) pitted prunes, halved
$^1/_2$ cup port or brandy
1 jar (28 oz.) mincemeat
2 cups chopped walnuts
pastry dough for a 9-inch double-crusted pie
beaten egg for glaze
sugar

Combine prunes and port or brandy in a covered container; let stand overnight. Add mincemeat and walnuts to prune mixture; set aside while you start assembling the pie. Spoon mincemeat filling into prepared pastry shell. Apply top crust and brush with egg; sprinkle with sugar. Bake in a preheated 425° oven for 10 minutes. Reduce heat to 375°. Continue baking 20 to 25 minutes until crust is golden and filling is bubbly. Cool on rack. Serve with whipped cream.

Macaroon Pie

4 egg whites
1 cup sugar
1 tsp. vanilla
1 tsp. baking powder
$^1/_4$ tsp. salt
1 cup graham cracker crumbs
$^1/_2$ cup shredded coconut
$^1/_2$ cup chopped walnuts

Beat egg whites until stiff. Beat in sugar gradually. Add vanilla. Mix remaining ingredients together and fold into beaten egg whites. Spread in a buttered and floured 9-inch pie plate. Bake in preheated 350° oven for 30 minutes. Top with whipped cream or vanilla ice cream. Serves 6.

Note: For a chocolate pecan pie, use chocolate wafers in place of graham crackers, and pecan nut meats in place of coconut and walnuts.

Summer Cherry Pie

 This pie is delicious and very refreshing. It's definitely worth making.

1 single, unbaked 9- or 10-inch pie shell
1 pkg. (3 oz.) cream cheese
2 Tbsp. milk
2 Tbsp. sugar
4 drops almond extract
1 pkg. (3 oz.) cherry Jell-O
1 cup boiling water
1 can (1 lb., 5 oz.) Comstock cherry pie filling

Line a 9- or 10-inch pie plate with the pastry. Bake pricked pie shell in a preheated 450° oven for about 12 minutes. (Watch carefully so it does not burn.) Cool. Combine cream cheese, milk, sugar, and almond extract. Spread over bottom of baked crust.

Dissolve Jell-O in boiling water. Cool until it's the consistency of syrup. Add cherry pie filling, and chill until partially set. Pour into pie shell, and chill until firm. Top with dollops of whipped cream.

Note: You may substitute any flavor Jell-O and pie filling. Strawberry is delicious.

Sylvia's Three-Berry Pie

Dough for a double-crusted 9-inch deep-dish shell

Filling:

Combine:

1^2/$_3$ cups each, blueberries, raspberries, and strawberries

Mix these with:

2 Tbsp. flour

1 cup sugar

2 Tbsp. lemon juice or orange juice

^{1}/$_8$ tsp. cinnamon.

Roll out the bottom crust generously enough to have a good overhang. Sprinkle with about 2 Tbsp. sugar; add the berry mixture, and dot all over with about 2 Tbsp. butter or margarine. Roll out top crust, fold in half, and fit over the fruit. Be sure to wet the rim of the bottom crust with water to seal the two crusts. Make a nice, thick rim so as not to lose any of the juice while the pie is baking.

Using your fingers, spread 2 Tbsp. butter-flavored Crisco over just the crust (not the rim). Sift a little flour over the Crisco, then brush crust with heavy cream. Last, sprinkle with sugar. Cut steam slits (I use about eight), and bake in a preheated 425° oven for 20 minutes. Lower temperature to 375° for about 20 more minutes or until you see juice bubbling in the slits you cut for steam. The crust should be nicely browned. There's nothing worse than an underbaked pie crust!

Note: The baking time is for fresh fruit. If you are using frozen berries, do not thaw. You will need to increase baking time to about an hour, and you may need to cover the top of pie with foil or parchment paper the last 15 minutes of baking time if the rim is getting too brown. Pies need to be watched closely—you don't just put them in the oven and forget about them. I always say, "You have to watch a pie as closely as you do your children; with tender, loving care."

Brownie Pie

1 single, unbaked 9-inch shell
2 cups chocolate bits, divided in half
$1/3$ cup butter or margarine
3 eggs
1 cup sugar
2 tsp. vanilla
$1 1/4$ cups flour
$1/4$ tsp. baking soda
$1/2$ cup chopped nuts

Melt 1 cup chocolate bits and butter in saucepan over low heat, stirring until smooth. Remove from heat; stir in eggs. Stir in sugar and vanilla. Add flour and baking soda; stir until smooth. Stir in remaining chocolate bits and nuts. Spoon into prepared pie shell. Bake in a preheated 350° oven for 40 to 50 minutes or until metal cake tester or toothpick inserted in center comes out slightly sticky. Serve with ice cream and a chocolate or caramel sauce.

Chocolate Fudge Pie
(No Nuts)

1 single, unbaked 9-inch pie shell
$1/2$ cup butter
3 sq. unsweetened chocolate
$1 1/2$ cups sugar
4 eggs
3 Tbsp. light corn syrup
$1/4$ tsp. salt
1 tsp. vanilla

Melt butter and chocolate over low heat; cool slightly. Beat in sugar, eggs, corn syrup, salt, and vanilla until just blended. Pour into pie shell. Bake in a preheated 350° oven for 45 to 60 minutes until nicely rounded (the top will crack a little and will sink down a bit as it cools. Serve warm or at room temperature with vanilla ice cream.

Nana's Chocolate Cream Pie

In a large saucepan, mix:

    1 $\frac{1}{2}$ cups sugar

    $\frac{1}{2}$ cup unsweetened cocoa or 3 squares unsweetened chocolate

    3 Tbsp. cornstarch

    $\frac{1}{8}$ tsp. salt

With a fork, stir in:

    3 egg yolks, one at a time.

With a wooden spoon, stir in:

    3 cups milk

Stir until all is well blended. Cook on low heat, stirring occasionally. Simmer on lowest heat, stirring constantly, for about 5 minutes. Remove from burner.

Add:

    1 Tbsp. butter

    1 $\frac{1}{2}$ tsp. vanilla

Allow to cool before filling a single, baked 9-inch pie shell. Refrigerate. Prior to serving, cover with whipped cream and garnish with shaved chocolate.

Chocolate Cream Pie

 This recipe is unusual, as it doesn't call for eggs. The pie is delicious and easy to make.

1 single, baked 9-inch pastry shell or crumb crust
$^1/_3$ cup unsweetened cocoa
1 $^1/_4$ cups sugar
$^1/_3$ cup cornstarch
$^1/_4$ tsp. salt
3 cups milk
3 Tbsp. butter or margarine
1 $^1/_2$ tsp. vanilla
sweetened whipped cream for garnish

Combine cocoa, sugar, cornstarch, and salt in medium saucepan; blend-in milk until smooth. Cook and stir over medium heat until mixture boils. Boil and stir for 3 minutes. Remove from heat; blend in butter and vanilla. Pour into pie shell; press plastic wrap onto surface. Chill 3 to 4 hours. Serve with sweetened whipped cream.

Note: This mixture will fill six custard cups if you prefer not to have a crust.

Lemon Cake Pie

1 single, unbaked 9-inch pie shell
3 eggs, separated
2 Tbsp. grated lemon peel
$^2/_3$ cup lemon juice
1 cup milk
1 $^1/_4$ cups sugar
$^1/_3$ cup flour
$^1/_4$ tsp. salt

Beat egg whites in a large mixing bowl until stiff peaks form; reserve. Beat egg yolks; beat-in lemon peel, lemon juice, and milk. Add sugar, flour, and salt; beat until smooth. Beat lemon mixture into egg whites on low speed until blended, about 1 minute. Pour into pastry shell. Bake in a preheated 350° oven until golden brown, 45 to 50 minutes.

Lemon Meringue Pie

1 single, baked 9-inch pie shell

Combine:
   1^1/2 cups sugar
   6 Tbsp. cornstarch or ^{3}/4 cup flour
   ^{1}/4 tsp. salt
Mix together and add to:
   3 slightly beaten egg yolks
Add:
   grated rind of one lemon
   6 Tbsp. fresh lemon juice
   2^1/4 cups boiling water

Mix well and cook in saucepan, stirring constantly on low heat until thick and clear.

Add:
   1^1/2 Tbsp. butter
Stir; cool slightly.

Turn into baked pie shell. Top with meringue, below.

Meringue:
   3 egg whites
   3 Tbsp. cold water
   1 tsp. baking powder
   6 Tbsp. sugar
   ^{1}/8 tsp. salt

Beat all together until meringue holds a peak. Cover top of filling. Bake in a preheated 375° oven for about 10 minutes.

Butterscotch Pie

1 single, baked 9-inch pie shell
1 cup firmly packed brown sugar
$^1/_4$ cup cornstarch
$^1/_2$ tsp. salt
3 cups milk
4 egg yolks, slightly beaten
2 Tbsp. butter
1 tsp. vanilla

In a large saucepan, blend together brown sugar, cornstarch, and salt. Stir milk into egg yolks, and slowly add to dry ingredients, mixing until smooth. Bring mixture to a boil over low heat and cook for two minutes. Remove from heat; add butter and vanilla. Let cool slightly while making meringue, below.

Meringue Topping:

4 egg whites
6 Tbsp. sugar
$^1/_2$ tsp. baking powder

Combine ingredients in mixing bowl; beat until meringue holds a peak. Spread over butterscotch filling, and bake pie in a 425° oven for about 5 minutes.

Note: You may substitute whipped cream for the meringue topping, but be sure to wait until filling has cooled completely.

Bars, Squares, Cookies & Fudge

Congo Bars

 I remember that when my mother made these, my two sons, Steven and Bryan, just loved them! Later, when I opened my shop, they quickly became a favorite and remained so for many, many years.

Melt in large stainless steel bowl or saucepan:

   1 cup (2 sticks) butter or margarine (I always use butter)

Add:

   1-lb. box (2^1/$_4$ cups) light brown sugar

   3 extra-large eggs

   1^1/$_2$ tsp. vanilla

Mix well with a spoon.

Add:

   2^1/$_2$ cups all-purpose flour

   ^{1}/$_4$ tsp. salt

   2 tsp. baking powder

Mix until well blended.

Add:

   2 cups real chocolate bits

   chopped pecans (optional)

Bake in a greased 15 x 10 x 2-inch pan for 20 to 30 minutes in a pre-heated 350° oven, or use two square 9 x 9 x 2-inch pans and bake for about 25 minutes (at 350°). You may also use a 13 x 9 x 2-inch pan and bake for about 25 to 35 minutes (again, at 350°).

Note: Before baking, I sprinkle the tops with chopped pecans, or you can save out a cupful of the chocolate bits and sprinkle those on top, which is what my mother did.

Nana's Blonde Chocolate Chip Pan Cookies

1 stick butter or margarine, softened
2 1/4 cups firmly packed brown sugar
3 eggs
2 3/4 cups flour
2 1/2 tsp. baking powder
1/2 tsp. salt
1 1/2 tsp. vanilla
1 to 2 cups chocolate chips
1/2 cup chopped nuts

Cream together butter (or margarine) and sugar; beat until smooth. Beat in eggs. Gradually add flour and other dry ingredients. Stir-in vanilla, chocolate chips, and nuts. Spread into greased 11 x 15-inch pan, and bake in preheated 350° oven for 20 to 25 minutes. Cool; cut into 35 bars.

My Mother's Fudge Cake Bars

2 cups all-purpose flour
2 cups sugar (or less)
1 tsp. baking soda
1/4 tsp. salt
1/2 cup cocoa
1 cup water or coffee

1 stick butter or margarine
1/2 cup shortening
2 eggs
1/2 cup buttermilk
1 tsp. vanilla

Sift together flour, sugar, baking soda, and salt. In a saucepan, combine cocoa, water, butter, and shortening. Bring to a boil. Cool slightly, then pour over dry ingredients in bowl. Beat until smooth. Blend in eggs; beat well. Add buttermilk and vanilla. Pour into greased and floured 13 x 9 x 2-inch pan, and bake in a preheated 350° oven for 25 to 35 minutes.

Frost in the pan with the frosting of your choice, and cut into squares. I always use my easy Fudge Frosting (page 49).

Fruit Bars

1 cup butter, melted
1 1/2 cups sugar
2 eggs
2 3/4 cups flour
1/2 tsp. baking soda
1/2 tsp. salt

1/2 tsp. nutmeg
1/2 tsp. cinnamon
1/2 tsp. cloves
1/4 cup buttermilk
1 cup raisins
1 cup currants

Melt butter in saucepan. Add sugar and eggs; beat well. Add dry ingredients and buttermilk; mix well. Stir in raisins and currants. Spread in a greased jelly-roll pan and bake in a preheated 350° oven for 20 to 25 minutes. Spread with glaze, below; cool in pan. Cut into 2 x 1-inch bars. Makes forty-five.

Lemon Glaze:

Mix 1 cup confectioners' sugar and 4 tsp. lemon juice. Add more of either ingredient as needed to adjust consistency of glaze.

Hermits

3/4 cup butter (1 1/2 sticks), softened
1 1/2 cups brown sugar
1/2 cup molasses
3 eggs
4 cups flour
1 tsp. salt
1 tsp. cinnamon
1 tsp. nutmeg

1/2 tsp. cloves
1/2 tsp. allspice
1/2 tsp. mace
1/4 cup strong coffee
1 cup raisins
1 cup currants
1 cup chopped nuts

In a large bowl, beat butter and sugar until light; beat in molasses. Add eggs, one at a time, beating thoroughly after each addition. Sift together the dry ingredients and add them alternately to first mixture with the coffee, beating until smooth. Fold in dry fruits and nuts. Pour into greased 15 x 10 x 1-inch pan. Sprinkle top with sugar before baking. Bake in a preheated 350° oven for about 20 minutes. Makes thirty-five bars.

Strawberry Meringue Bars

 These are quite special and are particularly appropriate for serving a large gathering.

Beat together:
   $3/4$ cup shortening
   2 egg yolks
   $1/3$ cup sugar
   $1/2$ cup flour

Spread in an ungreased 9 x 9 x 2-inch pan. Bake in a preheated 350° oven for 15 minutes. Remove from the oven.

Spread with:
   1 cup strawberry preserves

Beat:
   2 egg whites until foamy
Slowly add:
   $1/2$ cup sugar and beat until meringue peaks.
Fold in:
   1 cup chopped nuts

Spread meringue over preserves. Bake at 350° for 25 minutes. Cool pan on rack. Decorate with more preserves.

Banana Bars

 Packed in pretty tins, these make a nice holiday gift.

2 cups flour
1 cup sugar
$^3/_4$ tsp. baking soda
$^1/_2$ tsp. salt
$^1/_2$ tsp. cinnamon
1 cup mashed banana (two very ripe, medium-sized bananas)
1 (8 oz.) can undrained crushed pineapple
2 eggs
$^1/_2$ cup oil
1 tsp. vanilla
$^1/_4$ cup halved maraschino cherries

Combine flour, sugar, baking soda, salt, and cinnamon in a large bowl. Add bananas, pineapple with juice, eggs, oil, and vanilla. Mix until well blended. Stir in cherries. Pour into greased and floured 13 x 9 x 2-inch pan. Bake in a preheated 350° oven for 30 to 35 minutes. Cool for 30 minutes. Spread with creamy vanilla frosting, below.

Creamy Vanilla Frosting:

In saucepan, heat $^1/_4$ cup butter or margarine with 3 to 4 Tbsp. milk until butter melts. Remove from heat. Stir in 3 cups confectioners' sugar and 1 tsp. vanilla. Beat until smooth.

Sour Cream Banana Bars

These were very popular in my shop.

1 $^1/_2$ cups sugar
1 cup sour cream
$^1/_2$ cup butter or margarine, softened
2 eggs
1 $^1/_2$ cups mashed bananas
2 tsp. vanilla
2 cups flour
1 tsp. salt
1 tsp. baking soda
$^1/_2$ cup chopped nuts

Mix sugar, sour cream, butter, and eggs in a large bowl; beat on low speed for 1 minute. Beat in mashed bananas and vanilla on low speed for 30 seconds. Beat in flour, salt, and baking soda on medium speed for 1 minute. Stir in nuts. Spread in greased and floured jelly-roll pan measuring 15$^1/_2$ x 10$^1/_2$ x 1 inches. Bake in a preheated 375° oven until light brown—about 20 to 25 minutes. Cool. Frost with browned butter frosting, below. Cut into bars of about 2 x 1$^1/_2$ inches. Makes four dozen.

Browned Butter Frosting:

Heat $^1/_4$ cup butter or margarine over medium heat until delicately brown; remove from heat. Mix in 3 cups confectioners' sugar. Beat in 1 tsp. vanilla and 3 to 4 Tbsp. milk until smooth and of spreading consistency.

Note: This is easiest to spread with a spatula.

Apple Bars

1 tsp. vanilla
1 tsp. lemon extract
1 cup oil
2 cups sugar
2 eggs
3 cups flour
1 tsp. baking soda

1 tsp. cinnamon
$^3/_4$ tsp. cloves
$^3/_4$ tsp. nutmeg
$^1/_2$ tsp. salt
lemon peel
3 cups peeled, diced apples
1 cup raisins (optional)

In large bowl, beat vanilla, lemon extract, oil, sugar, and eggs. Sift flour, baking soda, all spices, salt, and lemon peel into above. Stir in apples and raisins. Bake in greased 15 x 10 x 1-inch jelly-roll pan in preheated 350° oven for about 45 minutes. Brush on glaze to desired thickness and cut into thirty-five bars.

Glaze:

2 cups (or more) confectioners' sugar
4 Tbsp. (or more) lemon juice or lemonade concentrate

Mix together well, using enough of both ingredients to make a thin, spreadable glaze.

Yummy Bars

1 cup peanut butter (creamy or crunchy)
$2/3$ cup butter or margarine, melted
1 tsp. vanilla
2 cups firmly packed brown sugar
3 eggs
1 cup flour
$1/2$ tsp. salt

Combine peanut butter and melted butter. Add vanilla, brown sugar, and eggs; mix well. Stir in flour and salt. Beat until smooth. Spread in greased and floured 13 x 9 x 2-inch pan. Bake in a preheated 350° oven for 35 minutes or until done.

Glaze:

$1/4$ cup chocolate chips
1 Tbsp. butter
$3/4$ cup confectioners' sugar
2 Tbsp. water

Melt chocolate and butter together. Add sugar and water and pour over bars when they are still warm but not hot; spread quickly. A large spatula is the tool to use.

Layered Coconut-Lemon Bars

 These are delicious! They make a nice gift when packed in a pretty tin.

Bottom:

> 2 cups flour
> $1/2$ cup butter or margarine
> $1/4$ cup brown sugar firmly packed or confectioners' sugar

Mix together with a fork until crumbly and press firmly into lightly greased 13 x 9 x 2-inch pan. Bake in a preheated 350° oven for 10 minutes. Cool.

Top:

> 3 eggs, well beaten
> 2 cups brown sugar (or less), firmly packed
> $1/2$ tsp. salt
> 1 cup coconut
> $1/2$ cup raisins
> $1/2$ cup walnuts
> 2 Tbsp. lemon juice
> 1 tsp. grated lemon zest

Mix ingredients for top, and pour over baked bottom crust. Bake combination for about 20 minutes in a preheated 350° oven. If desired, sift confectioners' sugar over the top.

Layered Coconut Bars

Shortbread Crust:

> 2 cups flour
> $1/2$ cup sugar
> $3/4$ cup butter or margarine
> $1/4$ tsp. salt

Blend with a mixer until crumbly. Press crust into bottom of a 13 x 9 x 2-inch pan. Bake in a preheated 350° oven for 10 minutes.

Coconut Topping:

- 1 1/2 cups brown sugar
- 3 large eggs
- 1 tsp. vanilla
- 1 cup chopped nuts (may be omitted)
- 2 Tbsp. flour
- 1/2 tsp. salt
- 1 1/2 cups coconut

Combine all topping ingredients. Carefully spread evenly over hot crust, above. Bake combination at 350° for 20 to 30 minutes. Cool in pan.

Note: Chocolate bits may be substituted for the chopped nuts.

Layered Oatmeal Bars

 For this recipe, you can use Date Nut Filling (page 57), jam, or canned Comstock fillings such as strawberry, blueberry, cherry, blackberry, etc., or jams. Mincemeat is delicious, too. Just use your imagination and try different alternatives.

Base and Topping:

- 2 sticks butter or margarine
- 2 cups flour
- 1 tsp. baking soda
- 1 tsp. salt
- 1 1/2 cups sugar (half white, half brown works well)
- 2 1/2 cups rolled oats

Melt butter or margarine. In a large bowl, combine flour, baking soda, salt, sugar, and rolled oats. Add the melted butter, and mix well. The result will be dry and crumbly. Press all but 2 cups of this mixture on the bottom of a greased 13 x 9 x 2-inch pan. Top with about 1 1/2 to 2 cups of filling. Sprinkle with the remaining crumb mixture; press gently with a spoon. Bake in a preheated 350° oven for 45 to 55 minutes or until brown. Cool. Cut into bars. Makes approximately three dozen, depending on how large you wish to cut them.

Pecan Fingers

 These layered bars are delicious.

Bottom:

$^3/_4$ cup butter or margarine
$^3/_4$ cup confectioners' sugar
1 $^1/_2$ cups flour

Mix together with a fork and press into a lightly greased 13 x 9 x 2-inch pan. Bake for 12 to 15 minutes in a preheated 350° oven.

Top:

2 eggs
1 cup brown sugar
2 Tbsp. flour
$^1/_2$ tsp. baking powder
$^1/_2$ tsp. salt
$^1/_2$ tsp. vanilla
1 cup chopped pecans

Combine all ingredients for top, and mix well. Spread this over baked bottom layer. Bake combination for 20 minutes in a preheated 350° oven. Cool and cut into twenty-four bars.

Pecan Pie Bars

Crust:

$^2/_3$ cup sugar
$^1/_2$ cup butter, softened
1 tsp. vanilla
1 egg
1 $^1/_2$ cups flour

Beat with mixer until blended. Press into an ungreased 13 x 9 x 2-inch pan, and bake in a preheated 350° oven for 10 to 15 minutes.

Top:

$^2/_3$ cup firmly packed brown sugar

$^1/_2$ cup corn syrup

1 tsp. vanilla

3 large eggs

1 cup pecans

Using a wooden spoon, beat together sugar, syrup, vanilla, and eggs. Stir in pecans. Pour over crust. Bake until set, 25 to 30 minutes. Cool completely. Cut into bars.

Hungarian Pecan Bars

Crust:

2 cups plus 2 Tbsp. flour

$^1/_4$ tsp. salt

$^1/_2$ cup sugar

1 cup butter, softened

2 egg yolks

1 Tbsp. brandy

Sift flour, salt, and sugar. Blend in butter; add the egg yolks and brandy. Pat evenly in greased 15 x 10 x 1-inch pan. Bake in a preheated 350° oven for 15 minutes.

Top:

$^1/_2$ cup sugar

$^1/_2$ cup firmly packed brown sugar

4 cups finely chopped pecans

$1^1/_2$ tsp. cinnamon

4 egg whites

In a heavy saucepan, combine sugars, pecans, cinnamon, and egg whites. Cook, stirring, over low heat until sugars dissolve. Increase heat and cook until mixture no longer clings to sides of pan. Spread on baked crust. Bake 15 minutes at 350°. Cool slightly. Cut into 3 x 1-inch bars. Dust with confectioners' sugar, if desired. Store in airtight container. Makes fifty.

Scotchy Peanut Bars

1 ⅓ cups flour
½ cup firmly packed brown sugar
⅔ cup butter, softened
1 cup sugar
1 cup light corn syrup
1 cup butterscotch chips
1 ¼ cups (12-oz. jar) peanut butter
3 cups corn flakes

Combine flour, brown sugar, and butter in mixing bowl. Mix at low speed until blended (mixture may be crumbly). Press into bottom of an ungreased 13 x 9 x 2-inch pan. Bake in a preheated 350° oven for 15 to 20 minutes.

Combine sugar and corn syrup in large saucepan. Cook over medium heat, stirring occasionally until mixture comes to a boil. Add butterscotch chips and stir to melt. Remove from heat and add peanut butter. Stir until melted. Stir in corn flakes. Spread over base. Cool. Frost with chocolate frosting (below) and cut into squares. Makes forty-eight.

Chocolate Frosting:

In a small pan, melt ½ cup chocolate chips and 2 Tbsp. butter in 1 Tbsp. milk. Add ¼ cup confectioners' sugar and ½ tsp. vanilla. Mix well.

Pumpkin Bars

2 cups flour
2 tsp. baking powder
2 tsp. cinnamon
1 tsp. baking soda
1 tsp. salt

4 beaten eggs
1 (16 oz.) can pumpkin
1 ½ cups sugar
1 cup oil
1 cup chocolate bits (optional)

Thoroughly beat all ingredients together, and spread in an ungreased 15 x 10 x 1-inch pan. Bake in a preheated 350° oven for 25 to 30 minutes. Cool. Frost with cream cheese frosting, below. Cut into thirty-six bars.

Cream Cheese Frosting:

>   1 (3 oz.) pkg. cream cheese
> $1/4$ cup plus 2 Tbs. butter
>   1 tsp. vanilla
>   2 cups confectioners' sugar

Mix everything until thick enough to spread on cooled bars in pan. Sprinkle with chopped nuts.

Date Bars

Filling:

> $2 1/2$ cups cut chopped dates
> $1/4$ cup sugar
> $1 1/2$ cups water

Cook until thick. Remove from burner and add:

> $1/3$ cup walnuts
>   1 tsp. vanilla

Coating:

> $1 1/4$ cups flour
>   1 tsp. salt
> $1/2$ tsp. baking soda
> $1 1/2$ cups rolled oats
>   1 cup firmly packed brown sugar
> $1/2$ cup butter
>   1 Tbsp. water

Blend flour, salt, baking soda, rolled oats, and brown sugar in a mixing bowl. Cut in butter until mixture is crumbly. Add water and blend in lightly. Press half into a greased 13 x 9 x 2-inch baking pan.

Spread with date mixture; cover with remaining oat mixture. Pat down lightly. Bake in a preheated 350° oven for 35 to 40 minutes or until lightly browned. Makes three dozen.

Note: You can substitute raisins or dried apricots for the dates. Add 2 Tbsp. jam to the filling for more flavor.

Frosted Ginger Bars
#1

$^1/_4$ cup butter or margarine
$^1/_4$ cup shortening
$^1/_4$ tsp. salt
$^1/_2$ cup firmly packed dark brown sugar
1 egg
$^1/_2$ cup molasses
1 tsp. vanilla
$^1/_3$ cup water
1 tsp. coffee powder
2 cups flour
1 tsp. baking soda
$1^1/_4$ tsp. ginger
$1^1/_4$ tsp. cinnamon
1 cup chopped raisins
$^3/_4$ cup chopped walnuts

Cream together butter, shortening, salt, sugar, and egg. Add molasses, vanilla, and water with coffee powder. Mix until well blended. Add the flour, baking soda, and spices. Beat together well. Fold in raisins and nuts. Spread in a greased 13 x 9 x 2-inch pan. Bake in a preheated 350° oven for 25 minutes. Do not overbake. Cool in pan. While warm, frost top evenly with coffee glaze.

Coffee Glaze:

Combine:
   $1^1/_2$ cups confectioners' sugar (or more)
   2 Tbsp. melted butter
   $1^1/_4$ tsp. vanilla
   $^1/_2$ tsp. instant coffee dissolved in 2 to 3 Tbsp. hot water
Mix until thin enough to spread over ginger bars (use a spatula).

Frosted Ginger Bars
#2

 These were very popular in my shop.

2 sticks plus 2 Tbsp. butter or margarine, melted
^{1}/3 cup molasses
1^1/2 cups sugar
2 eggs
1^1/2 tsp. baking soda
3 cups flour
^{3}/4 tsp. ginger
^{3}/4 tsp. allspice
1^1/2 tsp. cinnamon

Melt butter and add molasses, sugar, and eggs. Add all dry ingredients and mix well. Pour this into a greased jelly-roll pan, and bake for 20 to 30 minutes in a preheated 350° oven. Do not overbake. Makes forty-two bars.

Coffee Icing:

Melt 2 Tbsp. butter; mix in 1½ cups confectioners' sugar and 2 or 3 Tbsp. very strong, hot coffee. Mix thin enough to spread easily. Apply icing while bars are still warm from the oven. Cool before cutting.

Penuche Chews

^{3}/4 cup butter (1^1/2 sticks)
1^1/2 cups firmly packed brown sugar
^{1}/2 cup milk
2 cups flour
1 cup confectioners' sugar

1 tsp. salt
^{1}/2 tsp. baking soda
1 tsp. vanilla
1 cup chopped nuts

In a saucepan, combine butter, brown sugar, and milk. Bring to a boil over medium heat, stirring constantly; boil for 1 minute. Remove from heat and stir in remaining ingredients. Bake in a greased 15 x 10 x 1-inch pan in a preheated 350° oven. Bake 17 to 20 minutes or until lightly browned. Do not overbake. Makes sixty bars.

Chocolate Refreshers

 This was given to me many years ago by my friend Carolyn Robinson's mother, who is from Massachusetts.

1 ¼ cups sifted flour
¾ tsp. baking soda
½ tsp. salt
1 ¼ cups dates, cut
¾ cup firmly packed brown sugar
½ cup water

½ cup butter
1 cup chocolate bits
2 eggs
½ cup orange juice
½ cup milk
1 cup chopped nuts

Sift flour with baking soda and salt. Combine dates, brown sugar, water, and butter in a large saucepan. Cook over low heat, stirring until dates soften. Remove from heat, stir in chocolate bits, and beat in eggs. Add dry ingredients alternately with orange juice and milk. Stir in nuts. Bake on a jelly-roll pan or a large, greased cookie sheet with sides. Bake in preheated 350° oven for 25 to 30 minutes. Cool and spread on glaze. Cut into thirty-five bars.

Glaze:

1 ½ cups sifted confectioners' sugar
2 Tbsp. soft butter
1 to 2 tsp. grated orange rind
2 to 3 Tbsp. cream

Combine confectioners' sugar, butter, and orange rind. Blend in cream until of spreading consistency.

Basic Brownies

1 cup shortening
½ tsp. salt
3 squares unsweetened chocolate
4 eggs
2 cups sugar
1 ½ cups flour
1 tsp. baking powder
2 tsp. vanilla
2 Tbsp. corn syrup

Melt shortening, salt, and chocolate. Cream eggs and sugar and add to chocolate. Mix well. Add remaining ingredients. Stir well. Transfer batter to a greased 13 x 9 x 2-inch pan, and bake in preheated 350° oven for about 30 minutes.

Sylvia's Best Fudge Brownies

 Very popular with customers all over the United States!

Melt together in large saucepan:
   2 sticks butter or margarine (I use butter)
   4 squares unsweetened chocolate
   $1/8$ tsp. salt
Remove from heat and let cool for about 15 minutes.

Add to the cooled chocolate mixture:
   2 cups sugar
   2 tsp. vanilla
   3 extra-large eggs
Beat well with a spoon.

Add:
   $1\,1/3$ cups flour
   $1/2$ tsp. baking powder

Mix this in with a spoon. Do not beat; just be sure all ingredients are blended well.
Stir in:
   1 large cup mini-chocolate bits
   1 cup chopped nuts
OR
   2 cups (heaping) mini-chocolate bits (leaving out the nuts)

Transfer batter to a well greased 13 x 9 x 2-inch baking pan, and bake in a preheated 350° oven for 27 to 30 minutes or until done. Do not overbake!

Note: I use a disposable aluminum foil pan for this recipe. For some reason, the brownies seem to turn out nicer than when I use a regular metal pan.

Rocky Road Brownies

1 1/2 cups flour
1 1/3 cups butter or margarine
2 cups sugar
2/3 cup cocoa
1 tsp. baking powder
1/2 tsp. salt
4 large eggs
2 tsp. vanilla
2 Tbsp. corn syrup
2 cups chopped nuts
2 cups chocolate bits
3 cups miniature marshmallows

Combine first nine ingredients in a large mixing bowl. Mix on medium speed for 2 minutes. Stir in nuts, chocolate bits, and marshmallows. Spoon into two well greased 9 x 9 x 2-inch pans.

Bake in a preheated 350° oven for 20 to 30 minutes. Makes thirty-two bars.

Golden Brownies

3/4 cup butter
3/4 cup sugar
3/4 cup dark brown sugar
1 tsp. vanilla
3 eggs
1 tsp. salt
2 cups flour
2 tsp. baking powder
2 cups chocolate bits (12-oz. package)

Preheat oven to 350°. Cream together well the first six ingredients. Add the flour and baking powder; mix well. Fold in the chocolate bits (or sprinkle over the top before baking). Spread batter evenly in a well greased 15 x 10 x 1-inch pan. Bake for 30 to 35 minutes. Cool completely. Cut into 2-inch squares. Makes thirty-five.

Butterscotch Brownies

Melt:
  $1/2$ cup butter or margarine
Add:
  2 cups firmly packed brown sugar
  2 eggs
  $1 1/2$ cups flour
  2 tsp. baking powder
  $1/2$ tsp. salt
  1 tsp. vanilla
Mix well, then add:
  1 cup chopped nuts or chocolate bits or both.

Transfer batter to a greased 13 x 9 x 2-inch pan and bake for 20 to 25 minutes in a preheated 350° oven. Cut into twenty-four squares.

Easy Apple Squares

  $1 1/2$ sticks butter or margarine, softened
  2 cups flour
  $1 1/4$ cups firmly packed brown sugar
  $1/4$ tsp. salt
  $1 1/2$ cups graham cracker crumbs
  2 tsp. cinnamon
  1 tsp. baking soda
  1 (21 oz.) can Comstock apple filling

Mix together all but the last ingredient. Set aside 2 cups of the mixture, and pat the rest into a buttered 13 x 9 x 2-inch pan. Cover with apple filling. Sprinkle remaining 2 cups of crumbs over top of apple filling; pat down with a spoon. Bake in a preheated 350° oven for 30 to 40 minutes.

Note: These squares may be drizzled with lemon glaze, below, when cool.

Lemon Glaze:

Mix together 2 cups confectioners' sugar and enough lemon (or orange) juice (about 4 Tbsp.) to make a thin, spreadable glaze. Drizzle over the tops of bars.

Note: You can substitute any Comstock fruit filling for the apple; you can also make your own Cooked Fruit Filling (page 57).

Applesauce Spice Squares

 These were very popular in my shop. They're very easy to make and oh-so-tasty!

2 cups flour
$^1/_2$ tsp. salt
2 tsp. baking soda
$^3/_4$ tsp. cinnamon
$^3/_4$ tsp. cloves
$^3/_4$ tsp. nutmeg
$^1/_2$ cup soft butter or margarine
1 cup granulated sugar
1 egg
1 tsp. vanilla
1$^1/_2$ cups applesauce
1 cup nuts (optional)
1 cup light or dark raisins (optional)

Sift flour with the salt, baking soda, cinnamon, cloves, and nutmeg; set aside. In a large bowl, using a mixer at medium speed, cream the butter with the sugar until light and fluffy. Add the egg and vanilla; beat well, scraping down side of bowl with rubber spatula. At low speed, beat in flour mixture just until combined. Add applesauce, nuts, and raisins; stir with spoon until well mixed.

Turn into greased 15 x 10 x 1-inch jelly-roll pan. Bake in a preheated 350° oven for 25 minutes or just until surface springs back when gently pressed with fingertips. Sift confectioners' sugar over the top, or frost with a butter frosting and sprinkle with chopped nuts. Makes thirty-five bars.

Applesauce Squares

1 cup brown sugar
1 stick butter
1$^1/_2$ cups applesauce
$^1/_2$ tsp. salt
1 tsp. baking soda
2$^1/_3$ cups flour
1 tsp. baking powder
$^3/_4$ tsp. nutmeg
$^3/_4$ tsp. cinnamon
$^3/_4$ tsp. cloves
1 cup chopped raisins
$^1/_2$ cup nuts (optional)

Blend sugar, butter, and applesauce in large mixing bowl. Sift together and add dry ingredients. Mix well. Last, add raisins and nuts, if used. Put batter in a greased 13 x 9 x 2-inch pan or jelly-roll pan. Bake in a preheated 350° oven for about 25 minutes. Cool and glaze with Lemon Icing, below. Cut into squares.

Lemon Icing:

Mix 1 cup confectioners' sugar with 4 tsp. lemon juice; blend well, then spread on squares.

Raspberry Squares

 This is a recipe Priscilla Adams-Smith, my sister-in-law, gave me many years ago. It's delicious!

Cake:

  1 cup all-purpose flour
  1 tsp. baking powder
  $^1/_2$ cup butter or margarine
  1 egg
  1 Tbsp. milk
  $^1/_2$ cup raspberry jam

Sift flour and baking powder in bowl. Cut in butter with two knives until mixture looks mealy. Beat egg slightly and stir into flour mixture with milk. Mix well. Spread dough over bottom of greased 8 x 8 x 2-inch square baking pan; cover with a layer of jam.

Topping:

  4 Tbsp. butter or margarine
  1 egg
  1 cup sugar
  1 (4 oz.) can shredded coconut
  1 tsp. vanilla

Melt butter. Beat egg till frothy, then beat in sugar and melted butter thoroughly. Chop coconut into smaller pieces, mix with sugar-egg combination. Flavor with vanilla, and spread on top of jam.

  Bake in a preheated 350° oven for 30 minutes. Makes sixteen squares.

Layered Lemon Squares

Crust:

> 2 cups flour
> $3/4$ cup butter or margarine
> $1/2$ cup confectioners' sugar or $1/4$ cup firmly packed brown sugar

Mix together with fork or mixer until crumbly, then press firmly into lightly greased 13 x 9 x 2-inch pan. Bake for 10 minutes in a preheated 350° oven.

Top:

> 4 eggs
> $1\,1/2$ cups sugar (I use less)
> $1/3$ cup flour
> $1/3$ cup lemon juice
> $1/2$ tsp. baking powder

Combine eggs, sugar, flour, lemon juice, and baking powder; blend well with electric mixer for about 10 seconds, continually scraping sides of bowl. Pour over baked crust. Bake at 350° for 25 minutes or until golden brown. Cool and dust with confectioners' sugar.

Butterscotch-Coconut Squares

Melt:
> 2 sticks butter or margarine

Place in a large bowl.

With a mixer, blend in:
> $2\,1/4$ cups firmly packed brown sugar, or 1-lb. box
> $1/2$ tsp. salt
> $1/2$ cup sugar
> 4 large eggs
> 1 tsp. vanilla
> $1/2$ tsp. caramel flavoring
> $2\,2/3$ cups flour
> $2\,1/2$ tsp. baking powder

Beat until completely combined.

Stir in with a spoon:
    2 cups butterscotch bits
    1 cup chopped walnuts (or more)
    1 1/2 cups coconut

Divide batter between two greased 13 x 9 x 2-inch pans. Bake in a pre-heated 350° oven for 20 to 25 minutes. Do not overbake. Makes forty-eight bars.

Chocolate or Butterscotch Squares

4 cups chocolate (or butterscotch) bits
1/2 cup firmly packed brown sugar
10 Tbsp. butter
2 eggs, beaten
1 1/2 cups flour
2 tsp. baking powder
1/4 tsp. salt
2 tsp. vanilla
1 cup chopped nuts
2 cups miniature marshmallows

In a saucepan, melt 2 cups chocolate or butterscotch bits, brown sugar, and butter on low to medium heat, stirring constantly. Remove from stove. Add beaten eggs. Beat well. Mix in flour, baking powder, salt, and vanilla. Stir in final 2 cups chocolate or butterscotch bits, nuts, and miniature marshmallows. Spread in a greased and floured 13 x 9 x 2-inch pan. Bake in a preheated 350° oven for 20 to 25 minutes. Cool and cut into squares.

Toffee Squares

 These taste like Heath Bars.

1 1/2 cups flour
1/2 cup butter or margarine, softened
3 Tbsp. milk
1/4 tsp. baking soda
1/2 tsp. salt
1/2 cup chopped nuts
1/4 cup firmly packed brown sugar

In a mixing bowl, blend together with a fork until crumbly. Press firmly into ungreased 13 x 9 x 2-inch pan. Bake in a preheated 350° oven for 15 to 20 minutes or until golden brown. Prick all over with a fork.

3/4 cup butter
3/4 cup firmly packed brown sugar

In a saucepan, mix well and bring to a boil. Cook for 3 minutes. Pour over crumb base. Bake for 5 minutes in a preheated 375° oven. Let stand for 10 minutes.

3/4 to 1 cup semi-sweet or milk chocolate bits

Spread chocolate bits over warm surface. When chocolate is softened, spread it out like frosting.

Cut into thirty-two squares.

Pecan or Walnut Pie Squares

Crust:

  3 cups flour
  6 Tbsp. sugar
  $^3/_4$ cup butter or margarine
  $^3/_4$ tsp. salt

Grease bottom and sides of a $15^1/_2$ x $10^1/_2$ x 1-inch jelly-roll pan. With mixer at medium speed, beat flour, sugar, butter, and salt until mixture is crumbly (it will be dry). Press firmly into pan. Bake in a preheated 350° oven for 20 minutes or until golden. In the meantime, prepare filling, below.

Filling:

  4 eggs, slightly beaten
  $1^1/_2$ cups corn syrup, light or dark
  $1^1/_2$ cups sugar (or less)
  3 Tbsp. butter, melted
  $1^1/_2$ tsp. vanilla
  $2^1/_2$ cups chopped pecans or walnuts

In large bowl, stir eggs, corn syrup, sugar, butter, and vanilla until blended; stir in nuts. Spread evenly over hot crust.

  Bake in 350° oven for 25 minutes or until set. Cool before cutting into squares.

Peanut Butter Fudge

In a saucepan, combine:
    2 cups granulated sugar
    $^1/_2$ cup milk
    1 square unsweetened chocolate, shaved
Bring to a boil. Boil 6 minutes. Remove saucepan from stove.

Add:
    1 cup peanut butter
    1 cup Marshmallow Fluff
Beat these in.

Add:
    2 Tbsp. butter
    1 tsp. vanilla
    $^1/_2$ cup chopped walnuts

Beat quickly and turn into a buttered 9 x 9 x 2-inch pan. Chill, then cut into squares.

Creamy Peanut Butter Fudge

Bring to a boil:
    2 cups sugar
    2 cups brown sugar
    1 stick margarine
    1 cup evaporated milk
Cook for 3 minutes, stirring constantly. Remove from stove.

Add:
    1 cup peanut butter
    1 tsp. vanilla
Stir until creamy.

Pour into buttered 9 x 9 x 2-inch pan. Chill and cut into squares.

Erleen's Divinity Fudge

This is incredibly delicious!

3 cups sugar
$^1/_2$ cup light corn syrup
$^1/_2$ cup cold water
2 egg whites
1 tsp. vanilla

Place sugar, syrup, and water in a saucepan over slow heat. Stir only until sugar is dissolved. Cook until a little sample forms a soft ball when dropped into cold water.

Beat egg whites until stiff, add vanilla, and continue beating while you pour in half of syrup mixture.

Continue beating while you cook the rest of the syrup mixture, testing for doneness by dropping a little into a cup of cold water. It is done when it makes a hard ball that will crack when pushed against the side of the cup with the back of a spoon. Slowly add this cooked syrup to the egg whites and continue beating until candy loses its gloss and is thick enough to drop by the spoonful onto a buttered platter. Nut meats may be added before dropping from spoon.

The recipe makes at least 40 pieces of candy, which can be individually wrapped and stored in a tin.

Note: I sometimes use dark corn syrup, which gives the candy a pinkish tan color.

My Mother's Butter Cookies

1 lb. butter (no substitute)
1 cup confectioners' sugar
1 egg
4 cups flour

With electric mixer, beat butter for 10 minutes until white and creamy. Add sugar and egg; beat well. Sift flour, add to butter mixture, and continue beating. Finish by kneading for 5 minutes. If dough is too soft, refrigerate for 1 hour.

Pat dough down on board to a thickness of $^1/4$ inch, and cut with a cookie cutter. Place pieces on ungreased cookie sheet, $^1/2$ inch apart. Bake in a preheated 350° oven for 25 minutes or until lightly browned. Sift confectioners' sugar over cookies. Makes about three dozen cookies.

Butter Cookies, Version 2

 Here's another recipe for the same cookie. It uses the same process as above, except the flour is worked in by hand.

1 lb. sweet butter
$^1/4$ cup confectioners' sugar
1 tsp. vanilla
4 cups flour

With electric mixer, beat butter for 10 minutes until white and creamy. Add sugar and vanilla; beat well. Sift flour and add to butter mixture, working in by hand until it can be gathered into a ball. Finish by kneading for 5 minutes. Dough can be shaped by hand into crescents or round pieces, or rolled out to a thickness of $^1/4$ inch and cut with cookie cutters. Makes about three dozen cookies.

Bake in a preheated 350° oven for 15 minutes or until light, sandy color. Sift confectioners' sugar over cookies while still warm. Makes about three dozen cookies.

Note: The dough can also be rolled out into a rectangle and cut with a knife into diamond shapes, which is the way I remember them when I was very young.

Dimp's Butter Cookies

 This recipe comes from my patrons and friends Judy and Steven Levine, both doctors, from Los Angeles, California, and Rockport, Maine.

1 pound butter
1 cup sugar
3 egg yolks
1 tsp. vanilla
4 cups of sifted all-purpose flour

Cream butter well and add sugar gradually while continuing to cream. Add yolks, one at a time. Add vanilla. Add flour gradually, and mix until combined.

At this point, dough can be worked by hand or put into a cookie gun (if the dough is too soft, put it into the refrigerator for 15 minutes). To work by hand, roll dough into small balls, and use your thumb or the end of a wooden spoon to make an indentation in the tops.

To work with the cookie gun, use any disks you like. Extrude dough onto the cookie sheet, and follow baking directions, below. The cookie-gun cookies can be decorated with sprinkles, colored sugars, or icing. If not using colored sugars, sprinkle plain sugar on before baking.

Place cookies on an ungreased cookie sheet and bake in a preheated 350° oven for 15 to 20 minutes—until lightly browned around the edges. Let cookies rest for one minute before transferring them to a wire rack to cool.

When cool, fill hole in hand-shaped cookies with a little jam (I like seedless raspberry because the tartness makes a nice contrast with the sweetness of the cookie). Another choice is to fill the hole with chocolate icing. A pastry bag with a star tip works best for this. Makes about three dozen cookies.

Chocolate Drop Cookies

2 squares unsweetened chocolate

1 cup sugar

1/2 cup butter or margarine, softened

1 egg

1/3 cup buttermilk or water

1 tsp. vanilla

1 3/4 cups flour

1/2 tsp. baking soda

1/2 tsp. salt

1 cup chopped nuts

Heat oven to 400°. Melt and cool chocolate. Mix sugar, butter, egg, chocolate, buttermilk, and vanilla. Stir in flour, baking soda, salt, and nuts. Drop dough by rounded teaspoonfuls, about 2 inches apart, onto an ungreased cookie sheet. Bake until almost no indentation remains when cookies are touched (8 to 10 minutes). Immediately remove from cookie sheet. Cool; frost with Chocolate Frosting, below. Makes four and a half dozen.

Chocolate Frosting:

Melt 2 squares unsweetened chocolate and 2 Tbsp. butter or margarine over low heat; remove from stove. Beat in 3 Tbsp. water and about 2 cups confectioners' sugar until smooth and of spreading consistency.

Rice Krispies Chocolate Chip Cookies

1 cup butter or margarine

1 cup oil

1 cup sugar

1 cup firmly packed brown sugar

2 tsp. vanilla

1 egg

3 1/2 cups flour

1 tsp. baking soda

1 tsp. salt

1 tsp. cream of tartar

1 cup rolled oats

1 cup Rice Krispies

2 cups chocolate bits

3/4 cup chopped pecans (optional)

3/4 cup coconut (optional)

Cream together butter or margarine, oil, sugars, and vanilla. Add the egg and beat well. In a separate bowl, combine the flour, baking soda, salt, and cream of tartar. Add dry ingredients to creamed mixture and blend well. With a large wooden spoon, mix in the rolled oats, Rice Krispies, chocolate bits, nuts, and coconut, if desired.

Drop by teaspoonfuls onto greased cookie sheets. (Or, you can roll the dough in the palms of your hands to form 1-inch-diameter balls.) Bake in preheated 375° oven for 10 to 12 minutes. Makes ten dozen.

Best Chocolate Chip Cookies

 These are super good!

2 1/2 cups flour
1 tsp. baking soda
1/2 tsp. salt
1/2 cup butter or margarine, softened
1/2 cup shortening
1 cup firmly packed brown sugar
1/2 cup sugar
2 eggs
1 1/2 tsp. vanilla
2 cups chocolate bits
1 cup chopped walnuts or pecans

Sift together flour, baking soda, and salt. In a large bowl, beat butter and shortening with mixer on medium speed for 30 seconds. Add sugars and beat until fluffy. Add eggs and vanilla; beat well. Add dry ingredients to mixture, beating until well combined. Stir in chocolate pieces and nuts. Drop from teaspoon 2 inches apart onto an ungreased cookie sheet. Bake in a preheated 350° oven for 8 to 10 minutes or until done. Remove and allow to cool. Makes about fifty-five.

Oatmeal Chocolate Chip Cookies

1 cup butter or margarine, melted
1 cup firmly packed brown sugar
1 cup sugar
2 eggs, beaten
1 tsp. vanilla
1 cup rolled oats
1 cup corn flakes
2 cups flour
1 tsp. baking soda
1 tsp. baking powder
$1/2$ tsp. salt
2 cups chocolate bits

Blend together melted margarine and sugars in a large bowl. Beat eggs and vanilla; add to the sugar mixture. Mix in rolled oats and corn flakes. Sift together flour, baking soda, baking powder, and salt. Stir into oatmeal mixture. Stir in chocolate bits. Drop by teaspoonfuls onto ungreased cookie sheet.

Bake in preheated 350° oven for 10 to 12 minutes until light brown. Let cool for a minute before removing from cookie sheet. Makes five dozen cookies.

Basic Molasses Cookies

$3/4$ cup vegetable oil
1 cup sugar
$1/4$ cup molasses
1 egg
2 cups flour

2 tsp. baking soda
$1/2$ tsp. salt
$3/4$ tsp. cinnamon
$1/2$ tsp. allspice

Mix together oil, sugar, and molasses. Add egg and mix well. Add flour, baking soda, salt, cinnamon, and allspice; mix well. Drop by the teaspoonful; press with the palm of your hand. Bake on a lightly greased cookie sheet in a preheated 350° oven for 10 to 12 minutes. Makes about two dozen cookies.

Erleen's Soft Molasses Cookies

2$\frac{1}{2}$ cups flour
$\frac{1}{2}$ tsp. salt
1 tsp. baking soda
1 tsp. cinnamon
$\frac{1}{4}$ tsp. cloves
1 tsp. cocoa
$\frac{1}{2}$ cup shortening
$\frac{1}{2}$ cup granulated sugar
1 egg
$\frac{1}{2}$ cup molasses mixed with $\frac{1}{2}$ cup warm water

Sift flour with salt, baking soda, spices, and cocoa. In a large bowl, cream shortening and sugar; add egg and molasses/water mixture alternately with flour mixture. Drop by the teaspoonful onto a greased cookie sheet, and bake in a preheated 350° oven for about 10 minutes. Makes about thirty cookies.

Note: I sometimes add raisins to the dough.

Spicy Molasses Cookies

$\frac{3}{4}$ cup melted shortening
1 cup sugar
$\frac{1}{4}$ cup molasses
1 egg
2 cups flour
3 tsp. baking soda
$\frac{1}{2}$ tsp. salt
1 tsp. cloves
1 tsp. cinnamon
$\frac{1}{2}$ tsp. ginger

In a large mixing bowl, cream together the first four ingredients. Sift all dry ingredients, and add to creamed mixture. Mix well. Cover bowl and chill at least for 30 minutes. Roll level tablespoonfuls into small balls, then roll balls in granulated sugar. Place at least 2 inches apart on lightly greased baking sheets (allow ample space for spreading). Bake in a 350° oven for about 12 minutes. Makes about three dozen.

Gingersnaps

1 cup molasses
$^1/_2$ cup shortening
$^1/_2$ tsp. baking soda
3 cups flour
2 tsp. ginger
$^1/_2$ tsp. salt

In large saucepan, heat molasses to boiling point. Stir in shortening and baking soda. Remove from heat. Sift and measure flour; resift with ginger and salt. Stir into molasses mixture. Cover and chill dough. On a lightly floured surface, roll dough thin ($^1/_{16}$-inch thick). Cut into desired shapes. Place on lightly greased cookie sheet. Bake in a preheated 350° oven for 5 to 7 minutes or until no imprint remains when the cookies are lightly touched. Do not overbake. Remove from cookie sheet to cooling rack. Makes about six dozen cookies.

Super Gingersnaps

 This one comes from my best friend, Eleanor Weed Mathieson, who is like another sister to me. The recipe was given to Eleanor by my mother, Jennie Adams.

2 cups flour
1 Tbsp. baking soda
1 tsp. salt
$^3/_4$ tsp. ginger
$^3/_4$ tsp. cloves
$^3/_4$ tsp. cinnamon
$^3/_4$ cup shortening (I use half butter)
$^1/_2$ cup sugar
$^1/_2$ cup firmly packed brown sugar
1 egg
$^1/_4$ cup light molasses

Sift flour with baking soda, salt, and spices. Cream together shortening, sugars, and egg. Stir in molasses, then flour mixture. Drop by teaspoonfuls onto greased cookie sheet and flatten to circles. Bake in a preheated 350° oven for 10 minutes. Makes eighteen large cookies.

Erleen's Colossal Cookies

1 stick margarine
1$\frac{1}{2}$ cups granulated sugar
1$\frac{1}{2}$ cups firmly packed brown sugar
2$\frac{1}{2}$ tsp. baking soda
4 eggs
1 tsp. vanilla
1 (8 oz.) jar chunky peanut butter
6 cups rolled oats
1 (12 oz.) pkg. chocolate bits

In a large bowl, cream margarine, sugars, and baking soda. Add eggs, vanilla, and peanut butter; blend in. Add rolled oats and chocolate bits; mix well.

Drop by the teaspoonful onto a greased cookie sheet. Bake in a pre-heated 350° oven for 10 to 12 minutes. Makes about eighty cookies.

Oatmeal Raisin Cookies

3 eggs, well beaten
1 tsp. vanilla
1 cup raisins
1 cup shortening
1 cup firmly packed brown sugar
1 cup sugar
2$\frac{1}{2}$ cups flour
1 tsp. salt
2 tsp. baking soda
2 cups rolled oats
1 cup chopped pecans or walnuts

Stir together all the ingredients in a large mixing bowl. Shape dough into 1-inch balls. Place on ungreased baking sheets and flatten with fingers. Bake in a preheated 350° oven for 10 to 11 minutes. Do not overbake. Makes about three dozen cookies.

Soft Oatmeal Cookies

1 cup shortening
2 cups firmly packed brown sugar
1 tsp. salt
3 eggs
3 cups flour
1 tsp. baking powder
1 tsp. baking soda
1 tsp. cinnamon
1 cup sour milk or buttermilk
2 cups rolled oats
1 cup raisins
2 cups chopped nuts
1 cup chocolate bits (optional)

Cream together shortening, sugar, and salt until smooth. Add the eggs, one at a time, beating after each addition. Mix the flour, baking powder, baking soda, and cinnamon. Add this to the creamed mixture alternately with the sour milk or buttermilk. Stir in the rolled oats, raisins, nuts, and bits.

Either drop cookies from spoon or roll into $1^{1}/_{2}$-inch balls and flatten with your hands or with a fork. Bake in a preheated 350° oven for 12 to 15 minutes. Makes five dozen.

Crescent Cookies

2 cups flour
$1^{1}/_{2}$ cups ground pecans or almonds
$1^{1}/_{2}$ cups confectioners' sugar
1 cup butter, softened
$^{1}/_{8}$ tsp. salt
1 tsp. vanilla

In a large bowl, combine unsifted flour, nuts, 1 cup of the sugar, butter, salt, and vanilla. Blend well with an electric mixer. Divide dough into 36 balls. Form each into a crescent; place on ungreased cookie sheets. Bake in a preheated 375° oven for 12 to 15 minutes. Don't overbake. Sift remaining sugar over cookies. Makes about three dozen cookies.

Peanut Butter Cookies

1 cup shortening
1 cup peanut butter
1 cup sugar
1 cup firmly packed brown sugar
3 eggs
3 cups flour
2 tsp. baking soda
$^1/_4$ tsp. salt

Cream the shortening, peanut butter, and the sugars together. Add the eggs and blend well. Mix the flour, baking soda, and salt and beat into the creamed mixture.

Roll into 1$^1/_2$-inch balls and place 3 inches apart on ungreased cookie sheets. Flatten with a fork if desired. Bake in a preheated 350° oven for 10 to 15 minutes. Makes about forty cookies.

Mamma's Potato Chip Cookies

 This recipe was sent to me by Phyllis Anderson, a good friend of many years.

1 cup butter or margarine, softened
$^1/_2$ cup sugar
1 tsp. vanilla
$^1/_2$ cup crushed potato chips
$^1/_2$ cup chopped pecans
2 cups flour

Cream margarine, sugar, and vanilla. Add potato chips and pecans. Stir in flour and form into balls. Place on ungreased pan; press balls flat with a wooden cookie press or flat-bottomed saucer dipped into sugar. Bake in a preheated 350° oven for 15 minutes. Makes approximately three dozen small cookies.

Whoopie Pies

1 1/2 cups sugar
1/2 cup shortening
2 eggs
1 tsp. vanilla
1/2 cup sour milk
1/2 cup unsweetened cocoa

1/2 cup hot water
2 2/3 cups flour
1 tsp. baking soda
1 tsp. baking powder
1 tsp. salt

Cream sugar, shortening, eggs, vanilla, and milk. Make a paste of the cocoa and hot water. Cool, and add to the creamed mixture. Sift flour, baking soda, baking powder, and salt. Slowly add this to the first mixture, and blend well.

Grease cookie sheets, and drop batter by the tablespoonful, making sure you have an even number of pie halves. Don't crowd, as they will spread while baking. Bake 10 to 12 minutes in preheated 350° oven.

Spread about 1 Tbsp. of filling, below, on one half of each pie, and press second half on top. Makes about twelve to fifteen pies.

Filling:

In a saucepan, warm ½ cup milk over medium heat; using a whisk, blend in 2 1/2 Tbsp. flour, and stir until thick. Cool. In small mixing bowl, beat 1/2 cup shortening and ½ cup sugar. Add the cooked mixture, and beat until stiff and very creamy (like whipped cream).

Deanie's Whoopie Pies

 Deanie Hocking Ramsdell, my sister-in-law, gave me this recipe about forty years ago. My sons always loved these whoopie pies, so I made them often.

Melt:
  2 squares unsweetened chocolate
  4 Tbsp. shortening
Add:
  1 cup sugar
  1 1/2 tsp. baking powder
  1 1/2 cups flour
  3/4 cup milk
  1 tsp. vanilla
  1 egg

Chill dough for 1 hour. Put 1 tablespoonful at a time on a cookie sheet (no more than six in each batch, as they spread. Bake in a preheated 350° oven for 12 minutes.

Filling:

Part 1:
  2 Tbsp. butter
  2 Tbsp. flour
  1/2 cup milk

Cook until thick. Stir constantly as it thickens quickly. Chill thoroughly.

Part 2:
  1/4 cup butter
  1/4 cup (Crisco) shortening
  1/2 cup granulated sugar
  1 tsp. vanilla

Cream together all ingredients. Then add Part I, and beat like whipped cream. This will take a few minutes.

Put whoopie pies together with about 1 tablespoon of filling in center. Makes about twelve to fifteen pies.

Fruitcakes

Sherry Fruitcake

2 cups dates, pitted
2 cups pecans
2 cups cherries
1 cup mixed candied fruits
2 cups chocolate bits
1/2 cup cream sherry

6 eggs
1 cup sugar
2 tsp. vanilla
3 cups flour
2 tsp. salt

In a large bowl, combine dates, pecans, cherries, candied fruits, and chocolate bits. Add sherry; mix well and let stand for 1 hour, stirring occasionally. Place eggs in a large bowl, and beat with mixer until thick and lemon colored (about 5 minutes). Gradually beat in sugar and vanilla. Combine flour and salt; mix with fruit mixture. Fold in egg mixture. Transfer to greased and floured 9-inch tube pan. Bake in preheated 325° oven for about 1 hour. Cool in pan for 15 minutes. Remove cake from pan. Cool completely on wire rack.

Note: This fruitcake may also be baked in two loaf pans.

Light Fruitcake

1/2 cup butter
1 cup sugar
1 tsp. salt
3 eggs
2 cups flour

2 tsp. baking powder
1/4 cup orange juice
1 tsp. lemon extract
1 large jar candied mixed fruits

Cream together butter, sugar, and salt. Add eggs one at a time, beating after each addition. Add flour and baking powder alternately with orange juice and lemon extract. Add fruit last (it's not necessary to flour fruit).

Place batter in a well greased 9 x 5 x 3-inch loaf pan. Bake in a preheated 325° oven for 1 hour or until done. Cool thoroughly and wrap.

Sylvia's Dark Fruitcake

 This delicious recipe makes four to six cakes, depending on the size of the pans you decide to use.

In a large plastic bowl with a cover, mix together:
  1 cup liquor of your choice
  1 cup jam or marmalade
  1 tsp. nutmeg
  1 tsp. cloves
  2 tsp. cinnamon
  1 tsp. dry instant coffee
  1 tsp. vanilla
Add:
  1 cup dates
  1 cup dried apricots
  1 cup dried prunes
  1 cup candied pineapple
  1 cup light raisins
  1$^1/_2$ cups currants
  2 lbs. dark raisins
  1 cup candied cherries
  2 cups walnuts or pecans

Soak fruit and nuts in liquor mixture for 12 to 18 hours, stirring occasionally.

Cake batter:

Cream well:
  3 sticks butter and/or margarine
  1 lb. dark brown sugar (2$^1/_4$ cups firmly packed)
  6 extra-large eggs, added one at a time
Mix together:
  4 cups flour
  1 tsp. salt
  1 heaping tsp. baking powder
Add this to the creamed mixture with:
  1 tsp. vanilla.

Add cake batter to soaked fruit and nuts in bowl, and mix well. Grease loaf pans well, and line with wax paper. Fill pans about two-thirds full, and bake in a preheated 300° oven for 1$^1/_2$ to 2 hours.

When cakes are finished baking, pour about $^1/_4$ cup or more liquor over each top and leave in pans until it has been soaked up. Turn cakes out of pans, peel off wax paper, turn right side up, and allow to cool completely. Wrap well and refrigerate or freeze.

Notes: (1) You can use any kind of dried or candied fruit. (2) Soaking the cakes keeps them moist, so you may want to use more liquor. (3) You can also make this recipe in tube pans—perhaps two or three, depending on size.

Sylvia's White Butter Fruitcake

Let stand overnight in a large plastic bowl with a cover:
  4 cups pecans
  2 cups light raisins
  3 or 4 cups candied pineapple
  4 or 5 jars maraschino cherries, drained (leave whole)
  1 cup rum, brandy, or bourbon
  $^1/_4$ cup Amaretto

Cake batter:

Cream together well:
  3 sticks butter
  2 cups sugar
  1 tsp. almond extract
Add, two at a time:
  6 eggs
Beat well after each addition.

Combine:
  1 tsp. baking powder
  4 cups flour

Add dry ingredients to creamed mixture alternately with:
  $^2/_3$ cup pineapple juice or orange juice

Mix the batter with the fruit mixture. Thoroughly grease three 9 x 5 x 3-inch loaf pans lined with wax paper. Bake in a preheated 300° oven for $1^1/_2$ hours or until done. When cakes come out of the oven, leave in pans and soak with 1 cup liquor divided among the three. When liquor has soaked in, remove from pans, peeling off wax paper. Turn right side up, and let cool completely. Fruitcakes can then be wrapped for the freezer and saved for gift giving or for your own holiday parties.

English Fruitcake

one 16-oz. box (2 cups) currants
one 16-oz. box (2 cups) raisins
2 tubs (4 oz. each) citron
2 tubs (3^1/$_2$ oz. each) candied cherries, halved
1 can (8 oz.) walnuts, chopped
1 cup brandy or rum (divided in half)
1 cup butter
1 cup sugar
^{1}/$_4$ tsp. salt
1 tsp. vanilla
5 eggs
2 cups unsifted flour
1 tsp. baking powder
^{1}/$_2$ tsp. baking soda
^{1}/$_2$ tsp. nutmeg
^{1}/$_2$ tsp. cinnamon

Soak fruits and nuts in ^{1}/$_2$ cup brandy or rum until well mixed. Cream butter, sugar, salt, and vanilla; add eggs individually, beating each one well. Add flour and other ingredients alternately with second ^{1}/$_2$ cup brandy or rum.

Pour batter over prepared fruits and nuts, and mix well. Recipe will fill one 10-inch tube pan, two 9-inch tube pans, or two 9 x 5 x 3-inch loaf pans. Grease pans well, line with wax paper, and grease again before transferring batter. Bake in preheated 275° to 300° oven for 1^1/$_2$ to 2 hours or until done.

Note: To keep the cake extra moist, you can pour more liquor over it before wrapping. Or, you can substitute ^{1}/$_2$ cup grape juice for the brandy in the batter and pour that liquor over the cake when it comes out of the oven. Either way, this cake stores well in a cool place.

Dark Chocolate Fruitcake

 This is a very tasty cake if you like chocolate, and it stays moist for a long time.

one 16-oz.pkg. each, seedless and seeded raisins
$^1/_2$ cup mixed candied fruits
1 cup hot black coffee
1 cup purple grape juice
2 tsp. cinnamon
1 tsp. nutmeg
1 tsp. cloves
$^1/_4$ tsp. ginger
1 cup shortening or butter
2 squares unsweetened chocolate
1 cup maraschino cherries with the syrup
1 cup chopped nuts
4 eggs
2 cups firmly packed dark brown sugar
4 cups flour
1 tsp. salt
2 tsp. baking soda

Put raisins, candied fruits, liquids, and spices in a saucepan; bring to a boil. Simmer for 5 minutes; remove from heat, and stir in shortening and chocolate. Cool. Slice cherries, and add them to the first mixture with the syrup and nuts. Beat eggs slightly. Gradually add sugar, and beat until light and fluffy. Sift flour, salt, and baking soda together; add to the egg mixture alternately with the fruit mixture, stirring until well blended. Grease bottoms of two 9 x 5 x 3-inch loaf pans, line with wax paper, and grease again. Transfer batter.

Bake in a slow, preheated 300° oven for $1^1/_2$ to $1^3/_4$ hours. Let cakes stand in pans on rack until cold. Turn out, and peel off paper. Wrap cakes in cheesecloth moistened with sherry or brandy, and store for at least two weeks before cutting. Remoisten cheesecloth when necessary.

Note: Instead of wrapping the loaves with cheesecloth, I soak them in the pan with brandy when they came out of the oven, using about ½ cup for each. When the cakes are completely cold, I wrap them well and refrigerate or freeze them.

Christmas Cake

2 cups flour
$^1/_2$ tsp. baking powder
$^1/_4$ tsp. baking soda
1 tsp. cinnamon
$^1/_4$ tsp. nutmeg
$^1/_4$ tsp. cloves
1 $^1/_2$ cups currants
1 $^1/_2$ cups raisins
1 $^1/_2$ cups mixed candied fruits
1 cup candied cherries
$^1/_2$ cup ground almonds
4 eggs
1 cup sugar
$^3/_4$ cup melted butter
$^1/_2$ cup rum, brandy, or orange juice
3 Tbsp. lemon juice

In a large mixing bowl, stir together flour, leavening, spices, fruits, and nuts. Set aside. Beat eggs slightly with a fork. Add sugar, butter, the $^1/_2$ cup liquor or orange juice, and lemon juice; stir until combined. Blend egg mixture into flour and fruit mixture.

Pour batter into one 10-inch tube pan or two small loaf pans that have been greased, lined with wax paper, then greased again. Bake in a pre-heated 300° oven for 1 $^1/_4$ to 1 $^1/_2$ hours or until done. After baking, while the cake or cakes are still hot in the pan, you can pour either rum, brandy, or orange juice over the top (about $^1/_2$ cup). This keeps the cake(s) moist. When liquid is absorbed, remove cake(s) from pan. Cool completely on cake rack and wrap well. Either refrigerate or freeze.

Easy Fruitcake

6 cups walnuts or pecans
2 lbs. pitted dates
2 cups drained maraschino cherries (or more)

OR

3 cups walnuts
3 cups pecans
2 lbs. candied pineapple
1 lb. candied cherries
1 $^1/_2$ cups flour
1 $^1/_2$ cups sugar
1 tsp. baking powder
$^1/_2$ tsp. salt
6 eggs, beaten
2 tsp. vanilla

Put nuts and fruit in a bowl. Sift flour, sugar, baking powder, and salt over them. Mix with a spoon until nuts and fruit are coated. Beat eggs until foamy, and add vanilla. Stir into nut-fruit mixture until well blended. Put into one tube pan or two loaf pans that have been greased, lined on the bottom with wax paper, and greased again. Bake in a preheated 300° oven for 1$^3/_4$ hours.

Bourbon Fruitcake

2 cups white raisins
1 cup dried apricots
1 cup figs
2 cups candied mixed fruits and peels
$^1/_2$ lb. candied cherries
$^1/_2$ lb. candied pineapple
3 cups nuts
1$^1/_2$ cups bourbon (divided)
1 cup butter
1 cup sugar
1 tsp. salt
6 eggs
2$^1/_2$ cups flour
1 tsp. baking powder

Soak fruits and nuts in 1 cup bourbon overnight. Cream together butter, sugar, and salt. Add eggs to creamed mixture one at a time, beating after each addition. Mix flour and baking powder together; add to creamed mixture, blending well. Add this combination to soaked fruits and nuts, mixing well.

This will make four 7$^1/_2$ x 3$^1/_2$-inch loaf cakes or two 10-inch tube cakes. Put batter into tube pans or loaf pans that have been greased, lined on the bottom with wax paper, and greased again.

Bake in a preheated 300° oven for 1$^1/_2$ hours. Check for doneness with a metal cake tester or toothpick. When cakes are cool, pour the remaining $^1/_2$ cup bourbon over tops.

Note: 4 cups candied fruits can be used instead of figs and apricots.

Fruitcake with Simmered Fruit

In a large saucepan, combine:
    1 cup brown sugar
    $1/4$ cup molasses
    $1/2$ cup plus 1 Tbsp. shortening or butter
    2 cups seeded raisins
    8 oz. dates, chopped
    1 cup currants
    1 cup strong coffee
Bring this to a boil and cook for 5 minutes. Cool.

Stir in:
    1 egg
    2 cups flour
    $1/2$ tsp. baking soda
    1 tsp. baking powder
    1 tsp. cinnamon
    $1/4$ tsp. cloves
    $1/4$ tsp. salt
    1 tsp. vanilla
Mix well.

Grease a 9 x 5 x 3-inch loaf pan, line the bottom with wax paper, and grease again. Pour in batter and bake in a preheated 300° oven for about $1^1/2$ hours. Turn out onto rack, remove wax paper, and allow to cool.

Note: If you want nuts and candied fruits in your cake, add a cup of each to the cooked mixture.

Mincemeat Fruitcake

2 cups candied fruits and peels
2 cups prepared mincemeat
1 cup chopped walnuts
$^1/_4$ cup brandy or bourbon
$^1/_4$ cup butter or margarine, softened
$^3/_4$ cup firmly packed brown sugar
2 eggs
1 tsp. vanilla
2$^1/_2$ cups flour
$^1/_2$ tsp. baking powder
$^1/_2$ tsp. baking soda
$^1/_4$ tsp. salt

Combine fruits and peels, mincemeat, and nuts with ¼ cup liquor; set aside. Beat butter and brown sugar until fluffy. Add eggs and vanilla; mix well. Combine flour, baking powder, baking soda, and salt; add to sugar mixture. Add mincemeat mixture, and blend. Turn batter into greased and floured 12-cup fluted tube pan or 10-inch tube pan. Bake in a preheated 325° oven for 65 minutes or until done. Cool; remove from pan. To serve, drizzle with Brandy Icing, below.

Brandy Icing:

1 cup confectioners' sugar
2 Tbsp. brandy (or more)

Thoroughly blend sugar and liquor, adding more of one or the other as needed to make a glaze thin enough to drizzle over top of cake.

Puddings, Cobblers, & Other Desserts

Lemon Sponge Pudding

 In the summer of 1953, after Arnold and I were married, we lived at the Hockings' summer cottage in Tenants Harbor, Maine. That's where I was first introduced to this very refreshing, light dessert. It's just right after a hearty meal.

Combine:
 1 cup sugar
 2 heaping Tbsp. flour
 juice and grated rind of 1 lemon
 2 Tbsp. butter, melted
 2 egg yolks
Beat well.

Add:
 1 1/2 cups milk
Fold in:
 whites of 2 eggs, beaten stiff.

Pour mixture into baking dish and place in a pan of hot water. Bake in a preheated 350° oven until a knife comes out clean. (The sponge layer will come to the top, leaving the sauce on the bottom.) May be topped with whipped cream. Serves four.

Chocolate Bread Pudding

1 cup chocolate bits
3 cups milk, divided
3 eggs, slightly beaten
3/4 cup sugar
1/2 tsp. salt

1 tsp. vanilla
3/4 tsp. cinnamon
8 slices dry bread
1/2 cup broken walnuts

Melt chocolate bits in 1 cup milk over medium heat. Stir in remaining 2 cups milk; reserve. Combine eggs, sugar, salt, vanilla, and cinnamon; add to milk mixture. Trim crusts from bread and cut into 1/2-inch cubes. Put bread cubes into 1 1/2-quart buttered casserole. Pour milk/egg mixture over bread, making sure all cubes are saturated. Scatter walnuts over surface. Set casserole in a pan of warm water. Bake in a preheated 350° oven for 1 to 1 1/2 hours. Pudding is done when knife inserted in center comes out clean. When cool, serve with whipped cream or ice cream. Yield: six servings.

The Best Indian Pudding

 This was a favorite dessert with my sons when they were children. My husband loved it, too.

5 cups milk, divided
4 Tbsp. quick-cooking tapioca
4 Tbsp. cornmeal
2/3 cup molasses
1/2 cup sugar
2 Tbsp. butter
1 tsp. salt

Scald 4 cups milk, reserving the rest to be added during baking. Add tapioca and cook for 15 minutes, stirring continually. Mix together remaining ingredients in another bowl. Stir into tapioca mixture, and cook over hot water (in a double boiler) until thickened. Turn into a large, buttered baking dish. Cover and bake for 3 hours in a preheated 325° oven. Add the reserved 1 cup cold milk at the end of 2 hours. Serve with vanilla ice cream or whipped cream.

Grape-Nuts Pudding

6 eggs

$^3/_4$ cup sugar
$^1/_2$ tsp. nutmeg
$^1/_4$ tsp. cinnamon
$^1/_2$ tsp. vanilla
1 quart of milk
Grape-Nuts cereal to taste (I use about 1 cup)

Beat eggs enough to mix yolks and whites. Add next four items, and blend in milk. Stir well. Pour into a buttered baking dish. Set in a hot-water bath. Sprinkle Grape-Nuts on top of mixture. Bake in a preheated 350° oven for about 45 minutes or until done. Check with knife, as for custard.

Serve with whipped cream or ice cream. Recipe makes ten servings.

Strawberry Cobbler

$^2/_3$ to 1 cup sugar
1 Tbsp. cornstarch
1 cup water
3 cups strawberries with juices, if any
butter
cinnamon
1 cup flour
1 Tbsp. sugar
$1^1/_2$ tsp. baking powder
$^1/_2$ tsp. salt
3 Tbsp. shortening
$^1/_2$ cup milk

Mix sugar and cornstarch together; gradually stir in water. Bring to a boil and cook for one minute, stirring constantly. Add fruit and juices, if any. Pour into $1^1/_2$-quart buttered baking dish. Dot with butter. Sprinkle with cinnamon. Measure and stir flour, 1 Tbsp. sugar, baking powder, and salt in a bowl. Cut in shortening until mixture looks like meal. Stir in milk. Drop dough by spoonfuls onto hot fruit. Bake 25 to 30 minutes in pre-heated 400° oven. Serve warm with cream. Makes six to eight servings.

Note: Try this with any fresh fruit that's in season.

Sylvia's Apple Crisp

Crumb Base and Topping:

In a large bowl, mix:

  1 1/2 cups flour
  1 1/2 cups rolled oats
  3/4 cup sugar, brown and white
  1/2 tsp. cinnamon
  1 1/2 sticks melted butter or margarine
  1/4 tsp. salt
  1 Tbsp. water

Sprinkle a small amount of crumb topping on bottom of a greased 13 x 9 x 2-inch baking dish or a large rectangular casserole.

Filling:

  6 to 8 cups chopped or sliced apples
  1/4 cup sugar
  1/2 tsp. cinnamon
  1/4 tsp. nutmeg
  1 Tbsp. lemon juice
  1 to 2 Tbsp. water

Mix well, then place on prepared crumb base. Cover the apples with the remaining crumb topping, patting it down with the back of a spoon. Bake in a preheated 350° oven for 1 hour or until the top is golden brown. Serves ten. Serve warm with whipped cream or ice cream.

Praline Sundae Sauce

 This is the best caramel sauce I've ever tasted! Trying it is a must.

1 1/2 cups light brown sugar
2/3 cup light corn syrup
4 Tbsp. butter
1 small can evaporated milk or 2/3 cup fresh cream or milk
1 cup chopped pecans (I use halves)
1/8 tsp. salt

Mix first three ingredients, and heat to boiling point, stirring constantly. Remove from heat and cool. When lukewarm, add milk, pecans, and salt. Blend well. Stored in jars in the refrigerator, it keeps quite a long time. Serve over vanilla ice cream. Makes about 1 1/2 cups.

Note: You can leave out the nuts if you prefer.

INDEX